THE HESSIAN VIEW OF AMERICA
1776-1783

BY

ERNST KIPPING

PHILIP FRENEAU PRESS

MONMOUTH BEACH, N. J.

1971

Other titles in the Philip Freneau Press
Bicentennial Series on the American Revolution

THE BATTLE OF MONMOUTH
by Samuel S. Smith
LC No. 64-56379/ISBN 0-912480-00-9

THE BATTLE OF TRENTON
by Samuel S. Smith
LC No. 65-28860/ISBN 0-912480-01-7

AMERICAN MAPS AND MAP MAKERS OF THE REVOLUTION
by Peter J. Guthorn
LC No. 66-30330/ISBN 0-912480-02-5

THE BATTLE OF PRINCETON
by Samuel S. Smith
LC No. 67-31149/ISBN 0-912480-03-3

VALLEY FORGE CRUCIBLE OF VICTORY
by John F. Reed
LC No. 70-76769/ISBN 0-912480-04-1

FIGHT FOR THE DELAWARE 1777
by Samuel S. Smith
LC No. 74-130878/ISBN 0-912480-05-X

This Bicentennial Series
has been designed throughout by Paul R. Smith.
Photography by Daniel I. Hennessey.

Copyright 1971 by Philip Freneau Press
Library of Congress No. 72-161384
International Standard Book No. 0-912480-06-8

All rights reserved. No part of this book may be reproduced in any form without the permission of Philip Freneau Press, Box 116, Monmouth Beach, New Jersey 07750.

TABLE OF CONTENTS

FOREWORD

INTRODUCTION

CHAPTER I
THE HESSIAN TROOPS
Organization of Troops
Recruiting and Transport
Morale and Discipline
Desertion Among Hessians

CHAPTER II
THE AMERICAN COUNTRYSIDE
Ideas About America
Descriptions of Regions
Descriptions of Towns
Remarks on the Climate
View of the Countryside

CHAPTER III
THE AMERICAN PEOPLE
"Rebels" and German-Americans
Scorched Earth and Spies
Treatment of Loyalists
Negroes and Indians
Habits and Religion
Contact with Americans
Opinion of Americans

BIBLIOGRAPHY

ANNOTATIONS

APPENDIX

INDEX

FOREWORD

The author of the present volume began his studies of the American Revolution in the preparation of his doctoral dissertation at the University of Bonn. A portion of this study was published as a monograph in 1965 under the title *Die Truppen von Hessen-Kassel im amerikanischen Unabhaengigkeitskrieg 1776-1783,* which is concerned primarily with the logistics of the Hessian forces and their relationship to the British troops and their commanders during the American struggle for independence.

The more important part of this Bonn dissertation, certainly the more important from the American standpoint, deals with the opinions and views of North America as recorded by the Hessians in their letters and diaries. To prepare this part for publication in book form, Mr. Kipping felt compelled to study the source material that had been acquired by various libraries in the United States. He had already labored many long months in the Hessian State Archives at Marburg, searching for pertinent material in the official Hessian military records and the regimental journals. He had also made use of Captain Johann Ewald's diary, the most critical and most comprehensive Hessian diary (4 volumes) of the Revolutionary War, which is in the possession of His Excellency Friedrich Ferdinand, Prinz zu Schleswig-Holstein.

Aided by a stipend from the German Government, he spent most of 1964/65 in this country, working mainly in the manuscript divisions of the New York Public Library, the Library of Congress, and the William L. Clements Library (Ann Arbor), where the von Jungkenn Papers, a seven-volume collection of letters and diaries pertaining to the Revolution, are housed.

While working in the New York Public Library, Mr. Kipping met Mr. Samuel S. Smith, who was examining Hessian documents that might have some bearing on the battles of Trenton and Princeton. The two men came to respect each other as scholars and gentlemen (if I may use this somewhat overworked phrase), and finally Mr. Smith convinced the young German historian that he should write for the English-speaking public, since there would be more interest in the United States in a study such as he was planning than there would be in the German-speaking countries. Of course, this meant translating all the passages that were to be quoted, which alone was a sizable task, not because of the frequently spidery handwriting, but because of the oftentimes untutored syntax and the hurried writing which sometimes was necessary.

Reading the completed typescript of this study, I found that whenever part of a translated passage was a little "cockeyed," the original was so too. It then had to be dressed in a way which most nearly presented what the writer must have had in mind.

There is much interesting material on the Hessians and how they came to be auxiliary forces of the British, on the cultural and educational background of their officers, who documented what they saw and thought during the more than seven years they spent in this country, and on the many factors which brought about a change in their attitude toward America and its inhabitants, so that about six thousand of the approximately thirty thousand men settled in this country to enjoy the liberty, the attainment of which they were brought over to fight against.

This volume will be of interest not only to the historian of the Revolution, especially the cultural historian, but to everyone who likes to read about his country and its people as they were described by foreigners virtually two centuries ago.

Ann Arbor, Michigan   *B. A. Uhlendorf*

ARRIVAL OF BRITISH OFF STATEN ISLAND. *The British fleet from Halifax had been sighted approaching New York Bay during the forenoon of June 29, 1776. By 2 p.m., it was reported to General Washington that nearly one hundred vessels were at anchor within Sandy Hook Bay. On July 1, a number of British ships moved in closer and by nightfall, approximately fifty-five vessels were at anchor off Staten Island. On July 3, a landing was made on Staten Island. Admiral Richard Howe had not yet arrived with his fleet from Britain, which included the first division of Hessians. Then, on July 12, Admiral Howe's flagship, the EAGLE, was sighted approaching Staten Island. His fleet had dropped anchor inside Sandy Hook. As the EAGLE drew near to Staten Island, still under sail, Captain-Lieutenant Archibald Robertson of the British Engineer Corps climbed a rise above the water's edge on Staten Island and sketched this scene. Robertson titled his sketch, "View of the Narrows between Long Island and Staten Island with our Fleet at Anchor and Lord Howe coming in. Taken from the heights above the Watering Place Staten Island, 12th July, 1776." The Hessians remained near Sandy Hook until the 14th and 15th, when they sailed over to Staten Island and landed there. Courtesy New York Public Library; original sketch in Spencer Collection.*

INTRODUCTION

The military aspect of the Hessian participation in the American Revolution on the side of the British has been well documented. The human aspect of this German adventure has gone relatively unnoticed. It is the observations and opinions of chroniclers of these Hessian troops regarding the American people and the countryside, as revealed in their diaries and journals that is the main subject of this volume.

Participation in a war, in far-off America, was an adventure for the Hessians; and they looked on it with increased wonder, interest, and concern during their more than seven-year stay. This was true of the generals and down through the rank and file.

Recruiting in Germany, crossing the Atlantic, and the stay in a country about which most of them knew nothing, made lasting impressions on these men. The great majority of the troops, particularly the enlisted men, could not write; but those who could, mainly officers, described their impressions in diaries and letters, which convey their image of America.

Men of the Old World who saw Europe as the cradle and expression of man's spirit, came to the New World and measured it by these standards. Some showed subjectivity, and narrow-mindedness; others showed vividness, color, and imagination. All gave expression to the spirit of the outgoing eighteenth century.

These contemporary documents forming the basis of this volume consist largely of official military diaries of the Hessian battalions and regiments. The Hessian units which fought in America — there were twenty — had been ordered by the War Department in Cassel to record their experiences. Seventeen of the regimental or battalion diaries have been drawn upon in this study.

The personalities of the writers are imprinted on their diaries. Most of the writers were the regimental quartermasters, with the rank of captain. Because of differences in attitude, the value of the diaries vary considerably. Some of the writers made short work of their duties, taking note of nothing except the most unusual military events and the official business of their units. In these journals, there are almost no remarks on the countryside and the people of North America. In others, there are very impressive descriptions. They reported not only the movements of troops, but also recorded observations on the landscape, towns, and hamlets, on the inhabitants and their way of life, and on animals and vegetation. They explored the towns, rode out into the country, and wrote down all they saw.

The diarists had a good general education, augmented by their studies at cadet schools. These schools taught not only military subjects, but also philosophy, languages (Greek, Latin, French), history and geography. Some diarists had university training.

The few journals of pre-revolutionary civilian travelers to North America, which had been printed in Germany, had not been widely read, and the general knowledge of America was still meager. Due to this challenging lack of information, we are privileged to have available in German archives and publications (in addition to regimental diaries), a number of private diaries and many letters, parts of journals, and reports of Hessian officers describing America. The writers of these non-official documents did not have to follow instructions of the War Department.

CHAPTER I

THE HESSIAN TROOPS

Organization of Troops

More than 30,000 German soldiers fought on the British side in North America from 1776 through 1783. The number at any one time was approximately 20,000, which was only a little less than the number of British regulars. After the British Crown had concluded so-called "subsidiary treaties" with a number of German sovereigns, recruiting began in Hesse-Cassel, Hesse-Hanau, Brunswick, Anspach-Bayreuth, Waldeck, and Anhalt-Zerbst.

Landgrave Friedrich II of Hesse-Cassel provided the largest contingent of troops, more than 20,000 men going to America during the war. The Landgrave's son, Duke Wilhelm of Hesse-Hanau, who ruled his separate duchy independently, sent about 2,500 men to fight in North America. The duchy of Brunswick, under Duke Karl I and his son, Prince Karl Wilhelm Ferdinand, supplied about 6,000 men for the British service. The fourth German sovereign to conclude a "subsidiary treaty" with Great Britain was Markgrave Karl Alexander of Anspach-Bayreuth. He sent about 2,400 men to America. Prince Friedrich of Waldeck supplied almost 1,300 men from his small principality. The sixth German sovereign to send troops to America was Prince Friedrich-August of Anhalt-Zerbst. He furnished about 1,200 soldiers.

The first Hessian division landed on Staten Island on August 14 and 15, 1776; and, after the war, the last Hessian units departed for Germany from New York and Sandy Hook on November 25, 1783. They arrived in their homeland on April 20, 1784, after spending the winter in English garrisons.

Landgrave Friedrich II of Hesse-Cassel was the first German sovereign to agree to send troops to North America to fight for the British cause, as mercenaries. Although nominally a member of the Holy Roman Empire of the German Nation, the landgraviture of Hesse-Cassel was ruled independently by Friedrich II.

On February 12, 1776, a "subsidiary treaty" was ratified between Friedrich II and George III of Great Britain. This first agreement called for 12,000 men to be sent to North America. The corps was to consist of four grenadier battalions of four companies each, of fifteen infantry regiments of six companies each, of two jaeger companies of foot, and of supporting troops, such as artillery, engineers, etc.[1] The Landgrave was to supply equipment and accouterments.[2] Great Britain was to provide most of the artillery pieces and ammunition. In addition, each Hessian regiment was to take its own two field pieces.

The Landgrave established a War Department, or "War Commissariat" for recruiting, for providing supplies, change of personnel, etc. The office was directly under the authority of the Landgrave.

At a cost of about eighteen million pounds sterling, Great Britain helped speed up the preparations of getting the first Hessian units ready for their march to Bremerlehe (now Bremerhaven), where they were to embark for their crossing to North America.

The grenadier battalions, which were to prove highly effective for the conduct of war in America, did not exist as units of the Hessian line when the "subsidiary treaties" were signed. Therefore, the Hessian War Department combined the grenadier companies, of which each infantry regiment had one, to form grenadier battalions, consisting of four companies each.[3]

The first Hessian corps was organized in August 1776 in two divisions of two brigades each. A brigade consisted of three infantry regiments and one grenadier battalion.[4]

During the war, Great Britain and Hesse-Cassel signed several additional treaties to send Hessian troops to North America. By these treaties, the number of Hessian units increased from nineteen at the beginning of the war to twenty-one in 1783,[5] which was half of the total forty-two Hessian units.

During the course of the war, the increasingly effective Jaeger Corps was considerably enlarged. A treaty of December 11, 1776 stipulated that the corps get four additional companies of foot and two companies of mounted jaegers.[6] All of the Hessian cavalry, the engineer corps, the Guards and some fortress troops stayed in Hesse.[7]

The Hessian soldiers in America received the same pay as British troops. The costs of uniforms and equipment, which were sometimes supplied by the British High Command, had to be paid by the Hessians.[8] This form of management resulted, at times, in double supply, which caused some confusion during and after the war. Occasionally, neither the War Department in Cassel nor the Ministry of War in London felt responsible for furnishing supplies, so the Hessian soldiers suffered considerable privation.

The Hessian units were to get new uniforms and equipment every two years. Each regiment was to take care of maintenance. Repairs and new acquisitions had to be paid for by the paymaster's office of the Hessian High Command. This office was always short of money, and the Hessian generals dispatched many letters to Cassel requesting that this deplorable situation be improved.[9] Replacement uniforms and equipment were sent either in the ships of the recruit transports, or in ships loaded in German or Dutch ports, which joined British transports in the English Channel.[10]

In spite of efforts on the part of both sides, supply was never sufficient. The complaints of Hessian generals and commanders concerning uniforms, equipment, and armament never ceased. The main reasons for the poor servicing of the units were lack of coordination at the highest levels, the long supply line from Germany to North America, the loss of transports to both French and American raiders and warships, and the climate in North America.

Recruiting and Transport

With a total population of about 300,000, the principality of Hesse-Cassel had a relatively large army at the beginning of the struggle for American independence. Systematic and energetic recruiting augmented this force so that the first division could depart in the spring of 1776 and the second later the same year, the two divisions consisting of a total of about 11,600 men. In order to avoid critical consequences in agriculture, crafts, and the fabric of his country, as well as to save his own people from foreign service, Landgrave Friedrich II issued a decree late in 1776 to the administrative officials of his country. It proclaimed that he intended "with sovereign regard for the unavoidably necessary pursuit of agriculture" to replenish losses caused by troops sent to America mainly by attracting foreign recruits (i.e., non-Hessian Germans).[11]

The Hessian War Department organized a central office for this recruiting effort. Several German sovereigns and cities gave permission for recruiting in their territories. Recruiting centers were manned by officers, sergeants, and enlisted personnel of the Guard regiments, of the dragoon regiment von Schlotheim, of the dragoon regiment von Diemar, and of the dragoon regiment de Corps.

The recruiting personnel were ordered to solicit mainly young men for service in the Hessian units in North America. The printed instructions of the Hessian War Department to the recruiting officers permitted almost any means to attract recruits. Obscure machinations, bribery, "pressing" by making men drunk, and other tricks had been common methods of recruiting in Europe for centuries. The Hessians used them all, and invented a few new ones.

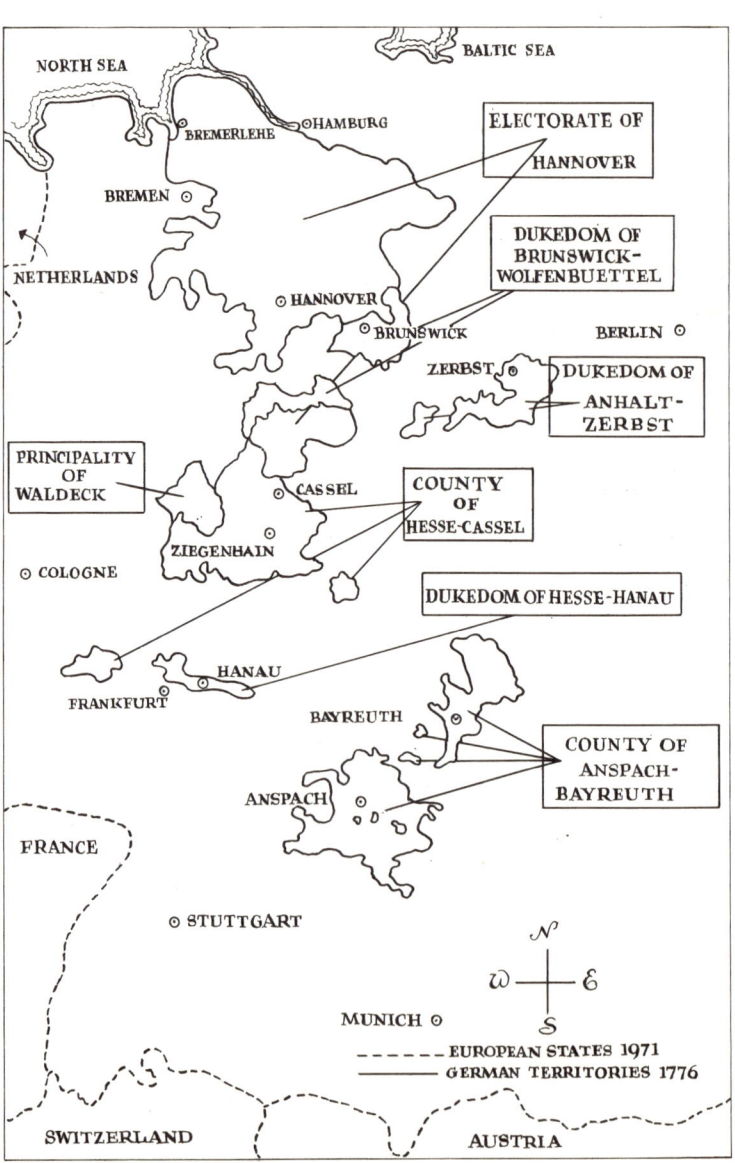

In the course of the war, Hessian recruiting became more and more difficult, due to the decline of the number of potential recruits in the regions around Hesse. There was also growing resentment in the German states against the use of German soldiers to fight in North America, which caused many young Germans to leave the Hessian recruiting areas. This situation forced the recruiting personnel to take old and physically infirm men in increasing numbers. When the British complained about the unfit recruits, the Landgrave issued stricter orders for recruiting.[12] But the general condition of the recruits improved very little.

For example, the Landgrave had to order the discharge of a 63-year-old man who could not walk erect; another he found "completely lame and limping because one of his legs was some inches shorter than the other."[13] Lieutenant General von Gohr, who was responsible for recruiting, consequently promised that henceforth stricter standards would be applied, and he would no longer recruit men over forty.[14]

Some strange results came out of the recruiting procedures. Colonel Ludwig Johann Adolph von Wurmb, the commander of the Hessian Jaeger Corps said in 1778 about a tailor from Cassel who was among the lately arrived recruits: "He is disabled and we cannot use him for service. He told us that he did not come over here to fight but to collect debts among the officers."[15]

Since the Hessian recruiting officers sometimes waylaid students who were on their way to a university, there were some highly educated soldiers among the Hessian rank and file. The nineteen-year-old Johann Gottfried Seume, who was to become a poet of some renown, was one of these students pressed into service. On the ocean and in camp near Halifax, N. S., he wrote his earliest known poems. His captain, H. C. Fenner, transmitted two of these in a letter to Colonel von Hatzfeld with the request that Seume be made a commissioned officer in view of his skills, his knowledge of languages, and especially his conduct.[16] (See B. A. Uhlendorf, "Some Unpublished Poems of J. G. Seume," *Germanic Review*, VII, 320-29, 1933.)

The complaints of Hessian officers in America about the quality of their recruits were especially frequent in the Jaeger Corps. Being an elite corps, it demanded higher standards than did the other Hessian units. Captain Johann Ewald of the jaegers complained bitterly about the later recruits as follows: "The officers were, with the exception of two French officers who had taken part in the war of the Confederacy of Bar against the king of Poland, men who had been detached from units that were left in Hesse. Noncommissioned officers and jaegers were mostly deserters from all nations, partly frustrated officers and noblemen, students of all disciplines, bankrupted men, tradesmen, and all sorts of adventurers."[17] On another occasion, Ewald called newly arrived recruits "dregs of society."[18]

The constantly deteriorating quality of recruits prevented effective training in the central recruiting camp at Ziegenhain. Mutiny and desertion were common at Ziegenhain in spite of many precautions.[19]

Poet Seume described the Hessian recruiting methods and life in the Hessian recruiting center as follows: "As a half prisoner I was brought to the fortress of Ziegenhain, where I found many miserable companions from all regions who were to go to America the next spring.... I surrendered to my fate and tried to make the best of it, bad as it was. We were stationed a long time in Ziegenhain, till a sufficient number of recruits was taken away from the plow, from the roads, and from the recruiting towns.

"This period of history is well enough known. Nobody was at that time secure from the handyman of the slave dealer.[20] Persuasion, tricks, fraud, and force, everything was legal. Nobody inquired about the means to this cursed end. Foreigners of all sorts were picked up, imprisoned, and sent off. My university matriculation certificate was torn up. This was the only instrument of my identity....

"Here was massed together a real medley of human beings; good ones and bad ones, and others who were alternately both. My comrades were another vagrant son of the muses from Jena, a bankrupt merchant from Vienna, a haberdasher from Hanover, a dismissed postal clerk from Gotha, a monk from Wuerzburg, a magistrate from Meiningen, a sergeant of the Prussian hussars, a discharged Hessian major from the fortress, and others of similar ilk. There was, naturally, no lack of entertainment...."[21]

Yet, there were some who volunteered for service in America. Many young men were eager for adventure and hoped to gain financially in the Hessian service. Others volunteered because it was the only way to get a free trip to America, and, once there, they would desert.

Claims of soldiers show that the Hessian army was very reluctant to fulfill the promises that were made when the men were recruited, and several commanders wrote to Cassel to obtain for their recruits the bounty that had been promised them when they signed the recruiting papers.

Many officers and enlisted men took their wives with them. Despite the fact that this created an additional problem for the commanders, the number of women among the troops rose steadily during the war. Especially, recruits who intended to defect in America in order to settle there, insisted on taking their wives with them. Colonel von Wurmb of the jaegers complained in August 1781 to Friedrich Christian Arnold, Baron von Jungkenn, Minister of State, that there were too many women coming over in the recruit transports. "This nuisance increases from year to year."[22]

Colonel Ludwig von Schallern of the Regiment von Seitz wrote the Minister of State, von Jungkenn, from Halifax, asking him to be godfather to his son, born August 17, 1781.[23] The commanders of a few Hessian recruit transports were compelled to send back to Hesse-Cassel some soldiers' wives because there was not enough room for them on board the ships, as reported in June 1782 by Major General Hans von Knoblauch from the *Charming Nancy* lying at Bremerlehe, ready to venture into the English Channel.[24]

ORIGIN OF GERMAN AUXILIARY TROOPS. *Shown here are the boundaries of the six German territories that made subsidiary treaties with Great Britain to fight in North America. Other main German cities in the 18th century are also shown for points of reference. The Electorate of Hanover is shown for the reason that George III of Great Britain was, at the same time, Duke of Hanover. The Electorate sent some regiments to fight in North America, but not as German auxiliaries. They were more or less incorporated into the British Army, and were stationed mostly in Canada. It is not uncommon to see all troops of German auxiliary troops referred to as Hessians. However, only the troops of Hesse-Cassel and Hesse-Hanau correctly may be called Hessians. The others should be referred to as Anspach-Bayreuthers, Waldeckers, etc. Possibly, the reason for this faulty reference is the fact that the Hessians furnished more than half of all German auxiliary troops in America.*

An account of Colonel Johann August von Loos pictured some difficulties inherent in the practice of permitting women to accompany their husbands on the voyage to America. Von Loos wrote in May 1776: "The wife of a soldier of one of my companies became ill this morning; an hour later she gave birth to a girl. (Since this child was born on English soil, she is more or less naturalized.) The military child bed lacks the arts of our modern doctors, and a simple company surgeon had to replace Dr. Stein. All our petted beauties of Cassel would be touched if they could see this poor creature. Instead of having nourishing broth, essences, and other needed things, she lies in a dark place, stretched on a mat; a mouthful of brandy, warm beer, and pepper were her only sustenance."[25]

After training in Ziegenhain, and subsequent review by the Landgrave, the recruits were dispatched as contingents, which left Hesse twice a year for America. They either marched from Cassel to the Weser River at Karlshafen, whence they went in river boats to the eventual embarkation at Bremerlehe; or they boarded river boats at Rheinfels and went down the Rhine to their final embarkation at Dordrecht, Holland.[26]

The transports, convoyed by British frigates, joined British recruit ships and crossed the Atlantic, arriving at Halifax, Nova Scotia, in sixty to seventy days, covering a distance of about 4,500 miles.[27] Many suffered from scurvy and some died, for food and water often became tainted during the crossing. With an average of about 900 to 1,000 recruits, every transport had about 130 to 200 men ill when it arrived in America, while about 30 to 40 had died.[28]

The first division of regular troops left Cassel on May 11, 1776; the second, later the same year; and the last transport of replacement recruits left on March 23, 1782.[29] In the course of the war seven contingents of recruits went to America, totaling nearly 7,000 men. An order issued by the Landgrave on February 3, 1783, put an end to recruiting for service in North America.[30]

Morale and Discipline

Morale and discipline of Hessian troops in North America presented an unusual problem. It was the first time that German soldiers fought so far away from Europe, in such large numbers. The great distance from Germany, the resulting homesickness, the new environment, the matter of obtaining much-needed supplies, and especially the unfavorable events of the war influenced the morale and discipline of the Hessian soldiers.

Soldiers of all ranks speak of homesickness in their letters. Many of them asked for more news from home. Major Carl Leopold Baurmeister wrote: "For four and one-half months the Hessian troops have received no news from the Fatherland. Convinced, as we are, that we are graciously and warmly remembered, we are at a loss to understand why we have had no assurance of it for so long. We have been sending letters with every packet. I myself find much comfort in writing, for I cannot think day after day of our distant homeland without becoming sentimental."[31]

An enlisted man of the Regiment de Corps asked in two letters for news from his parents and brothers and sister in Hesse. Assuring everybody in his hometown that all soldiers of the village were alive and well, he continued in one of the letters: "My dear parents and brothers and sister. I do not know what to do because you do not write. Do you think that I am dead or did you forget me entirely? Or are you glad that I left you...?"[32]

The high-ranking generals had a less personal interest in news from Germany. Lieutenant General Friedrich Wilhelm von Lossberg complained in January 1779 that he received the last mail in May 1778.[33] Lieutenant Colonel Friedrich Wilhelm von Wurmb wrote that he was grateful for having been sent the '*Altonaer-Zeitung* (a Hamburg newspaper), from which he learned about events of the War of the Bavarian Succession.[34]

Lieutenant Colonel Johann Friedrich von Cochenhausen reported that there were no letters from Hesse in the last mail, which arrived in New York in February 1779; there were only packages. "These were probably sent by mounted mail service and the other part of the mail, that crawls by coach on lame feet, arrived too late in London."[35]

LIEUTENANT GENERAL WILHELM VON LOSSBERG. *It was this officer (at the time of this painting a major general) who in 1779 was complaining about not receiving enough mail from home. Von Lossberg was then colonel of the von Lossberg regiment. However, von Lossberg never actually commanded his regiment in America, but was assigned brigade duties. Von Lossberg rose steadily in rank, and in May 1782, became commander in chief of all Hessian forces in America. Courtesy State Art Collection, Kassel, Castle Wilhelmshoehe.*

Since effectiveness and a high combat readiness of a combined army depended on strict discipline, the Hessian High Command tried from the beginning to enforce uncompromising order among the troops.[36] Breaches of discipline were most common in wintertime partly because of long confining winterquarters in America. Hence, disciplinary actions by the commanding generals were frequent during these months. They were almost never necessary in times of combat.[37]

The Hessian High Command strictly enforced discipline and good behavior in occupied cities. In line with this desire to make a good impression, officers had orders to furbish their uniforms and have their hats pressed.[38] They were to take part in parades, as they did in Cassel, which would encourage the rank and file to imitate this good conduct.

Nevertheless, there were the usual cases of misconduct found in all armies. Two lieutenants of the Regiment Landgraf accused each other of theft. They were both imprisoned until a Hessian court-martial tried the case.[39] Some officers of the Regiment von Wissenbach were heavy drinkers and were unfit for duty for long periods of time.[40]

Sometimes misconduct by officers in America would have been considered acceptable practice in Germany. When punishment had to be given to wrong-doing civilians in occupied areas, some Hessian officers were found to be giving lashings, until it was ordered that this form of punishment was not to be practiced in America as it had been in Germany.[41]

In certain cases, the reaction of the Hessian High Command to undisciplined behavior of officers was quite severe. Some were dishonorably discharged from the army and sent back to Germany. This was the fate of two ensigns, Strasser (Regiment von Dittfurth) and Vockroth (Regiment von Porbeck), because they did not stop drinking in spite of repeated warning and punishment.[42]

While there was but little looting by the soldiers who arrived in the first and second divisions, many of the recruits sent over subsequently were guilty of this crime. Lieutenant General Wilhelm von Knyphausen, the second commanding general, reported to the Landgrave in the winter of 1777-1778 that many of the soldiers imprisoned because of looting and robbery were new recruits.[43] In the same winter the commander of the Regiment von Mirbach felt compelled to prohibit the cutting-down of fruit trees and fences for firewood, not to mention the tearing-down of houses also for the purpose of firewood.[44]

Some acts of theft were a result of the bad food or lack of food. An order of the Regiment von Mirbach of October 1777 provided regulations regarding taking food supplies from local residents. The order stipulated that cattle was to be purchased and not to be taken away by force of arms.[45] The usual punishment for not obeying this, and similar orders, was "30 or more strokes with a stick on the backside."[46] Lieutenant General von Knyphausen had ten men of Stirn's brigade run the gauntlet for marauding after the landing at Elk Ferry, Md.[47]

Lieutenant General von Knyphausen reported to the Landgrave that the English High Command had ordered all officers to enforce strict discipline, and von Knyphausen vouched to do the same in the Hessian corps.[48] It was unusual for the Hessian High Command to sentence a soldier to death by hanging, only two cases being recorded in the Hessian papers. Lieutenant General von Lossberg, who succeeded von Knyphausen as commander in chief, ordered the hanging of two soldiers of the Regiment de Corps in the summer of 1782 in New York because they were found guilty of highway robbery and wounding a civilian.[49]

The British more often praised than censured the conduct of Hessian troops. Major Baurmeister, for example, reported on August 27, 1777, that the British Lieutenant General William Howe, commended the commander of the Hessian Jaeger Corps and Colonel Carl Emil Ulrich von Donop for maintaining excellent discipline among their troops.[50]

When provisions ran low, the Hessians, as did the British, sent out foraging parties, the officers of which carried requisitions. Cruel acts of violence occurred, however, when British-Hessian and American foraging parties met and engaged each other. Many farmhouses and barns went up in flames during these encounters.[51] Farm buildings of militant "rebels" were frequent targets.[52]

Generally, the Hessians were well thought of by the British. Major General Alexander Leslie, in November 1780 on board the *Romulus* in Hampton Roads, wrote to Lieutenant General Henry Clinton in New York: "The Hessian [are] a most respectable corps."[53] On the occasion of the embarkment for home of the last Hessian troops in November 1783, the then British Commander in Chief, Lieutenant General Guy Carleton, wrote to the Landgrave: "I cannot let slip the occasion to testify to Your Serene Highness, the sense I justly entertain...of the exemplary behavior of the Hessian troops...during the time that I have had the honour to command this Army."[54]

Desertion Among Hessians

The Hessian High Command listed 2,949 deserters during its expedition to North America.[55] The number of men who really defected, or did not return to Germany after the war, was much greater. Many Hessian prisoners were not exchanged either during the war or after the peace treaty. Some had already settled in the country when Hessian officers went in search of them so that an exchange might be effected. These men were not included in the official desertion lists.

The number of these defectors can only be estimated, but based on prisoner returnee statistics available in some regiments, there is reason to assume that their number ran between 2,000 and 3,000. Further, many of the more than 900 officially discharged men, also stayed in America. These were mostly commissioned officers and sergeants who had married, or were about to marry, daughters of American Loyalists. It is therefore estimated that more than 6,000 Hessians remained in America.

The rate of defection was very much higher than during similar commitments of German troops in Europe, mainly among the rank and file. One reason was that the sojourn in North America put more stress upon the common soldiers than did similar service in Europe, not because of more severe fighting but rather because of one important factor peculiar to this war. A great number of these subjects of German feudal sovereigns were confronted with a revolutionary war toward which they were not altogether unsympathetic. This was true particularly of the underprivileged, found mainly in the rank and file.

During the first two years of the war there was little desertion: 66 in 1776 and 109 in 1777.[56] The rate increased to

422 in 1779, and remained at approximately that level during the rest of the war. The primarily native Hessian troops, while they were victorious, ordinarily kept their oath of allegiance and did not defect. When the battle losses rose and new recruits arrived, and privations occurred more often, the American propaganda was effective enough to bring about a degradation of troop morale, which increased desertions.

The first time there was significant evidence of this was during the fatiguing march of the British-Hessian Army from Philadelphia to New York through New Jersey in the summer of 1778. Early the following winter, even the commander of the Hessian Jaegers, Colonel von Wurmb, admitted to the high rate of desertion among his elite troops.[57] Colonel von Wurmb reported further that many of the later recruits thought that they would have the same good winter quarters in North America as in Cassel, "and because they were housed in poor shelters here, they deserted."[58] Some of these recruits, secured by questionable methods, even deserted on their march from Cassel to the ports of embarkation in Germany or Holland. Some were assisted by relatives, and, on occasion, by soldiers of the covering party.[59]

A report by Hessian Headquarters in America commented on the problem as follows: "Most of the recruits, mainly foreigners [non-Hessians], behave very badly and defect at the first opportunity; therefore, we cannot use them on outposts. Many of them may have intended to take advantage of the chance of free passage to this country, and finally to quit Europe. They would have had to work about four years to pay the costs of their crossing. We must take into account that the condition of those regiments which have already had great losses and which will have even greater losses if they stay a long time will greatly deteriorate by having recruits join them."[60]

At the end of the war very little could be done to control desertion, especially in the units stationed in the southern provinces, e.g., at Savannah, Ga., and Charleston, S.C.[61] American propaganda, plus persuasion by German-Americans, and the fear of not being exchanged after the peace treaty, were probably the main reasons for defecting after actual hostilities had ceased.[62] Major Baurmeister repeatedly reported on the growing desire of the troops to desert: "Collecting the prisoners and preventing desertion in the regiments stationed here [in New York] will require double care and watchfulness.

"Immediately after the rumor of an impending peace, some men escaped here and there. They have been captured and severely punished, but since the promises are so alluring, it will be difficult to prevent all desertion."[63] Two weeks later, April 29, 1783, Baurmeister noted: "We are fortunate in having prevented desertion so far, although the Jaegers have had some, as well as the Landgraf Regiment, which is stationed in Brooklyn in an open place on an open island, where it cannot be sufficiently guarded."[64]

Lieutenant General von Lossberg, reported on some measures by which the Hessian Headquarters tried to control desertion. In the beginning, soldiers who were recaptured were punished by having to run the gauntlet or even by being hanged.[65] Later the units sent out patrols to catch deserters. The British and Hessians often used Negroes and Indians for this purpose. These "hunting detachments" were paid two guineas in Savannah for each captured deserter. In retaliation, Congress punished these Negroes with death by hanging when they were caught by the Continental Army.[66]

In garrisons and camps, the enlisted troops were closely guarded after the war so that there were fewer opportunities to defect. Deserters sometimes returned to their units voluntarily. Either they could not get used to their new surroundings, or they took advantage of the several general pardons proclaimed during and right after the war. In the Jaeger Corps, for example, twenty-one men returned after a general pardon in the year 1781.[67]

As early as August 1776, when rumor spread among the Americans that the British were engaging the services of German troops to fight against them, Congress tried to entice these troops to desert. Mainly American citizens of German descent were the most active in carrying out these plans. They drafted proclamations and pamphlets and spread them among the Hessian and other German troops. Small portions of tobacco for the clay pipes of German soldiers were packed in these handbills and distributed among them. The handbills, printed in German, enumerated the various privileges of American citizenship and promised fifty acres of land to all deserters who intended to settle as American citizens.[68] Knowledge about the American offers was spread in Germany not only by Hessian soldiers, many of them invalids who had returned from America, but also by the American diplomatic mission in Paris.

Later in the war, General Leslie wrote to General Clinton about the results of the American propaganda in the Hessian Regiment von Knoblauch, stationed in Savannah, Ga.: "From Colonel Clarke's letters to me, I find the Hessian Regiment has been there[69] too long, they desert fast, and I am afraid little dependence is to be put in them; I shall for this reason be under the necessity of withdrawing them, I am very much at a loss whom to send to replace that corps. I am sorry to observe that when the Hessian troops are sent to outposts, desertion takes place; they being so long here has been the means of their forming too many connections. And the enemy have taken every care to encourage desertion as much as in their power, this together with the assistance of their friends within our walls enables them to seduce the foreigners, [non-Hessians] from the encouragement they give them."[70]

Calls for desertion, drafted and signed by two of the few deserted Hessian officers, proved especially effective. Major Baurmeister wrote disdainfully of such a deed by the defected Ensign Fuehrer of the Regiment von Knyphausen and Ensign Kleinschmidt of the Regiment von Woellwarth, who had deserted in August 1778.[71]

Prisoners of war presented another Hessian problem. As early as 1777, the Americans had started to release Hessian prisoners to work on farms and at trades. Eight hundred and sixty-eight rank and file Hessians who had been captured at Trenton, December 26, 1776, were marched to Pennsylvania, specifically to the so-called Pennsylvania-Dutch country.

Many of the prisoners were confined in camps only a short time. Beginning September 10, 1777, and continuing through November 20, three hundred and ninety-seven prisoners were released to work for civilians. The areas where most of the prisoners worked were the neighborhoods of Lancaster, Lebanon, Reading, and York. (See Appendix)

After the war, all prisoners including those who had been "farmed out", as well as escapees, were offered new inducements to stay in America. They could either join the Continental Army or start farming with 200 acres of land, one cow and two pigs. Such help was promised in proclamations (in the German language), which were freely distributed in Hessian prison camps.[72]

When the prisoners did not respond as expected, American officers turned to other means. The prisoners were asked to pay for food and lodging during their captivity, which most of them did not have the means to do. Fearing an uncertain future, often with wives and children,[73] many decided to enlist in the Continental Army.[74] Prisoners who did not wish to join the Continental Army were released upon payment of 80 dollars, after which they became American citizens upon signing an oath of allegiance.[75]

The step from prisoner of war to prospective American citizen was made by signing, before witnesses, a paper which read: "I .... do acknowledge myself a Prisoner to the United States of America, and pledge my Faith and sacred Honour, that I will not say, do, or cause to be said or done, any Thing that may injure the Welfare of the said States, by holding any Correspondence with the Enemies thereof, or those in any Way opposing the measure entered into by them, in Defense of their Liberty, or that may in any shape be construed so to be, that I will go to .... and there, or within one mile therof, remain until exchanged. In testimony whereof, I have hereunto set my Hand .... this .... day of ...."[76]

In an effort to cut down post-war defections, the Hessian High Command tried to contact all Hessian prisoners and supply them with uniforms and money until exchanged.[77]

Reports of Major Baurmeister from New York in June and July of 1783 showed the extent of American propaganda and its results among the Hessian troops. "The captive troops of Lord Cornwallis's Army continued to arrive on Staten Island till the 27th of May. Major Scheer[78] is greatly worried about having had 240 deserters since his departure from Frederickstown, namely, 136 in the Erb Prinz Regiment and 104 in von Bose's.... These desertions are due only to the scattering of printed invitations and previous persuasion on the part of the inhabitants, who have resorted to every possible inducement. Of von Knyphausen's Regiment, 140 men have not yet returned. Lieutenant Colonel du Puy[79] arrived from Philadelphia within the last few days. In spite of every effort, he did not succeed in obtaining the release of the men bought out of captivity. Moreover, there is no hope of the escaped prisoners ever returning, unless they come in voluntarily after the proclamation of the general pardon.

"Brigadier General Clarke is before Congress demanding that the articles of peace be carried out in every detail in this respect; one-sixth of the prisoners of Bourgoyne's army have not come in yet because of such reasons. The state of affairs is serious in every respect, for while the prisoners are being begged for and gathered, the standing army has more desertion than ever before, which reports clearly show."[80]

In July 1783 Major Baurmeister traveled from New York to New Jersey and Pennsylvania to look into the situation of the German soldiers who were employed here and there. At a meeting in Philadelphia with Assistant Secretary of War, Major William Jackson, Major Baurmeister heard the American view concerning the exchange of these men. "(1) The War Council has no jurisdiction over the Hessian, Brunswick, and Hesse-Hanau soldiers who have been sold out of imprisonment to the inhabitants. (2) Whether the soldiers are released or not depends entirely upon the owners of these men and upon the desires and intentions of the foreign soldiers. (3) No German soldiers may return to the British Army unless the owners are reimbursed in cash for their outlay...."

Elias Boudinot, President of Congress, made the following statement after confirming the decisions of Major Jackson: "...if His Excellency General von Lossberg wanted to get possession of these prisoners, the Americans would permit it in return for a cash payment of 30 pounds Pennsylvania currency per man;...and if the German soldiers really desired to return, America held open her arms to people of all nations, in welcome and protection."[81]

After this meeting with Boudinot, Major Baurmeister visited all Hessian prison camps in Pennsylvania and New Jersey. Due to his efforts, some Hessian soldiers returned to their units. With the date of embarkation for the first Hessian units set for August 12, 1783, the Hessian High Command stopped all efforts to exchange its prisoners. There was no renewed attempt to exchange Hessian soldiers until shortly before November 25, 1783, when the last Hessian contingent under the command of Major General von Gosen was to leave Sandy Hook for home.

CHAPTER II

THE AMERICAN COUNTRYSIDE

Ideas About America

Toward the end of the eighteenth century, Germany was a conglomerate of territorial and political units. There were about 300 states of varying size, which were allied by a variety of treaties and agreements, either with each other or with powers outside of Germany. All these territories were nominally united under the Crown of the Emperor of the Holy Roman Empire of the German Nation; but the empire lacked the power to establish political unity of Germany.

This decentralization of political power was an important factor in establishing numerous capitals, that competed with each other as centers of culture. Never before, and not since, has Germany produced so many giants in literature, music and philosophy.

In this political and intellectual atmosphere of Germany, the first news about a smoldering rebellion in North America was received with little concern. A few German newspapers reacted with a sort of curiosity, probably because news of America was thought to be of some interest to their readers. Most newspapers tried to be neutral on the subject, but all expressed hope that the differences between Great Britain and her North American Colonies could be solved peacefully.

As early as the summer of 1774, a far sighted editor of the "Augsburgische Postzeitung" wrote: "This irritating subject, which, it was believed, could be terminated without bloodshed, will without doubt cost the lives of many Europeans and Americans.... All letters from America agree that the inhabitants are preparing for a case of emergency and that they seem to be determined to defend their steps to obtain their charter, privileges, and liberties. Therefore I expect sad events, if a peaceful settlement cannot be found."[82]

By spring of 1776, after Great Britain had concluded "subsidiary treaties" with several German sovereigns, Frederick the Great of Prussia, aware of the political frustration in Germany, and of Prussia's role in the eventual attainment of German unity, criticised Landgrave Friedrich II of Hesse-Cassel. In a letter to his closest intellectual friend, Voltaire, he said: "If the Landgrave had come out of my school, he would not have sold his subjects to the English as one sells cattle to be taken to the slaughter house.... Such conduct is motivated only by selfish greed. I pity the poor Hessians who will end their lives unhappily and uselessly in America."[83]

The youthful Friedrich Schiller, Germany's greatest dramatic poet of the classical period, raised his voice in protest against this human traffic in his social drama *Kabale und Liebe*, which appeared in print in 1784, the year most of the German troops returned home. In Act II, Scene 2, he describes a spectacle where men who refused to follow the call of their sovereign and raised their voices were shot in the market square, where crying children ran after their fathers who were recruited, where bride and bridegroom were separated by swords, where the aged were forced to join the lines or flung their crutches after the young men who marched out of the town. And the young men turned their heads at the town gates and shouted: "God help you, wife and children! Long live our father, the Duke! We shall be back for the Day of Judgment!"

Newspapers of the German states that had concluded "subsidiary treaties" with Great Britain saw these treaties from a different viewpoint. They dwelled on the reciprocal relations between Great Britain and these states and the need of alliances with the British Crown. King George III was, at the same time, Elector of Hanover (in 1815 he became the first King of Hanover) and, therefore, one of the most important sovereigns in the Holy Roman Empire. Landgrave Friedrich II of Hesse-Cassel was a close relative to George III. The Landgrave's first wife, Princess Mary, was a daughter of King George II. Prince Carl Wilhelm Ferdinand of Brunswick, the son of Duke Carl I of Brunswick, was a brother-in-law to George III.

Songs of War

There are sixty songs, dating from the period 1773 to 1776, which reflect the feelings of the common people about the American War and the participation of German troops in this war. There is one, consisting of twenty-one four-line stanzas, which, in a way, attempts to justify the sending of Anspach-Bayreuth auxiliary troops, because England had supported German sovereigns against France. The author had in mind the Austrian War of Succession (1740-1748). During this war, mainly between Austria and Prussia, English, Hanoverians, and Hessians, under George II, defeated the French in the battle of Dettingen in 1743.[84]

Other songs appealed more directly to the emotions of potential recruits; in fact, some had a distinct propaganda flavor. One is quite derisive. Freely translated, titled simply "Folk Song," it reads:

> "Hurrah! we go to America,
> Good night to you, Germania
> Present your arms, you Hessians,
> The Landgrave will inspect you!
>
> Good bye, Landgrave Friedrich,
> You pay for gin and beer!
> For the arms and legs we lose,
> England will pay you.
>
> You lousy rebels, you,
> Beware of us Hessians!
> Hurrah! we go to America,
> Good night to you, Germania."[85]

Excerpts from the other songs will illustrate the tenor of these poetic effusions.

> "Come with us to America,
> The land of plenty.

LANDGRAVE FRIEDRICH II OF HESSE-CASSEL. *Friedrich II ruled his landgraviate from 1760-1785. He is shown here as a general with field-marshal's baton in his hand. The flags in the background show the Hessian lion. The "FL" in the flag and on the flag standard stand for "FRIEDRICH, LANDGRAF." This painting is by Johann Heinrich Tischbein (the older one), and was completed in 1773. Courtesy State Art Collection, Kassel, Castle Wilhelmshoehe.*

Silver and gold, land and wealth,
What you are looking for in the world,
You will find in America.
Yes, everything you are looking for,
You will find in America."[86]

———

"Why do you cry, my beloved, with a sad face,
We are all in search of a fortune,
In the past we have had only small pay,
But now honor and gold are awaiting us[....]

And if Heaven will lead us back home,
We will have glory, ducats and fortune;
But if we die as brave soldiers there,
Earth will cover us as well as it does here."[87]

———

"Good bye, my Hesse, good bye!
Now comes America,
And our fortune is growing —
Mountains of gold are there!
Further, in enemy country,
The hand will take what we lack,
This is indeed a much better life."[88]

———

"There were states ten and three
Wanting to be from England free,
Wanted to be Respublica,
A free State America!

There will be fighting soon,
We hear England is mobilizing already,
Has acquired auxiliary troops,
For high pay and wages.

So in the New World,
There will also be war
Where there are humans on earth,
Peace will turn into dispute."[89]

In the course of war, some German newspapers tried to give unbiased accounts of events in America and to understand its ideological and political background. The *Muenchner Zeitung* published reports of the American side and printed American comments, but rather declined to give its approval.

In the autumn of 1776, the Munich paper said: "The printed news from America of August shows us clearly that each colony makes laws for itself, installs admiralty courts, appoints governors, who have to be changed each year if it does not please the inhabitants to re-elect them. They nominate judges, mobilize an army, and abolish the authority of the King completely. Thus they act in all colonies, but always with the greatest care that each colony obeys the orders of the General Congress in Philadelphia to secure the general defense of the liberty of America."[90]

As early as 1774, an article in the *Augsburgische Postzeitung* reported on the German immigrants in America and on their enthusiasm for the cause of independence: "There are 25,000 Germans in the Province of Pennsylvania alone. Most of them have fought during the last war[91] and are now citizens, landowners, and farmers, and have declared to take up arms if the country is denied the liberty which they had sought to find in the New World."[92]

In spite of all apparent political reservations about the War of Independence and its aims, the same paper could not conceal a certain sympathy for the Americans when it reported in June 1776 from the Spanish port of Cadiz: "There is often an opportunity to talk with Americans, who arrive here from Boston and other cities of the English Colonies. They cannot describe with words how extraordinary a revolution is going on in that part of the world, and how little the discontented there fear the frightful British force of arms which is moving towards them."[93]

Descriptions of Regions

The war in North America was an adventure for Hessian officers and men, which drastically shaped their lives. One Hessian officer wrote: "The order to fight was welcome to the war-minded Hessian, but the fate of a voyage across the sea and of a campaign on a foreign continent awakened anxious expectations. In the opinion of subordinate officials, the North Americans were cannibals, and a crossing of the Atlantic was rarely a happy one. This was true even at a time when it was seldom decided to make a voyage at a moment's notice. One weighed the cause, made a decision, formally said farewell to his possessions, made his will, then locked the house and departed."[94]

Upon arrival in New York Harbor, the units of the first Hessian division were exhausted and weakened by the long crossing. Nevertheless, they were exuberant in reporting their first impressions of the country. Lieutenant Bardeleben wrote in his diary, "When we sailed into New York, we passed a long shore that was covered with hills and fir trees [the New Jersey Highlands and Staten Island]....There was a small piece of open sea to the south [Sandy Hook Bay], a heavenly sight indeed."[95] Quartermaster Heusser noted in the journal of the Regiment (Alt) von Lossberg: "The inhabitants of this island [Staten Island] say that this is the most fertile soil in America and call it the Garden of America. But the people of New Jersey do not admit this and claim their own province to have this appellation."[96]

Quartermaster Sartorius of the Regiment Prince Hereditary recorded: "This countryside is so pleasant; I do not remember having seen anything like it before. The shores are well cultivated, and the landscape becomes even more pleasant as we get close. All the houses are built of stone and stucco painted white and covered with shingle roofs. This is the reason it looks like a camp from a distance. The houses are separated from each other, and the fields are separated with fences. The livestock looks good, and it is evident that they have enough fodder."[97]

Captain Johann Hinrichs of the Jaeger Corps described the same scene: "Staten Island is a hilly country with nice forests of fir trees. They can be seen at a distance of two hours out at sea. The island is not extensively cultivated. The soil is very fertile. Peaches, chestnuts, nuts, apples, pears, and grapes grow wild in between rose and blackberry bushes. The climate and the soil are surely the most beautiful, healthy, and the most pleasant in the world....Everything looks the same as it does at home; the same bushes, the same woods, though the leaves are larger and the wood stronger because the soil is more fertile."[98] The regimental journal of the Grenadier Battalion Koehler noted: "Staten Island is well cultivated and has many mountains and fresh springs."[99]

Captain Hinrichs later described upper Manhattan Island: "New York Island is the most beautiful I have ever seen. There is not an unnecessary tree, branch or blade of grass on this island. Productive hills alternate with arable flat land, meadows, and gardens. Houses on the hillsides along the river are a most lovely sight. They are all painted white. There are porches around the first floor, a balcony, and a lightning rod.[100] They are all built and furnished in good taste."[101]

A report to the Landgrave in the journal of the Hessian Corps summarized the impressions of the New York area:[102]

"Staten Island consists mostly of hills, whose soil is a sort of copper color. This causes the water to taste of vitriol. Long Island, which also has poor water, has many hills to the west as well as to the north, although it also has many plains. Furthermore, there are good roads which are not paved because the soil consists of gravel. The houses and farms along the water and most houses in the villages are spread around as in Westphalia except those that are grouped around a church. Everybody has his own plot of ground, garden, meadows, and forest, fenced in by rails with four of them fixed horizontally one foot apart between two posts. Sometimes the fields or meadows are fenced in with stones that are loosely piled on top of each other. In this way they clear their fields.

"All houses on Staten and Long Island are built lightly in Dutch style, but the houses on Long Island are nicer. They consist mostly of one, seldom of two floors, and are made of wood and brick, with a shingled roof. The roof has an overhang of about four or six feet. This covers a porch, with a rail one to one and a half feet high, that runs around the house, giving cover from rain. The barns are separated from the houses by about a hundred yards. Next to the barn is another building with stables for horses and cattle during winter."

Quartermaster Carl Bauer noted in the journal of the Grenadier Battalion Koehler about upper Manhattan Island: "This region seems to be very fertile...There is still much cattle raising in spite of the war. The inhabitants, of whom one can see only a few in their houses, seem to have been very happy before this fight began. The houses are nice and regular, not like our style of farmhouses at home. Most of the fine furniture in the deserted houses was ruined."[103]

The Hessian soldiers did not step onto the American mainland until they crossed over to New Jersey beginning November 25, 1776. Their time had been spent mainly on Staten, Long, and Manhattan Islands. Now, they found themselves marching through New Jersey, from near Fort Lee to Trenton. On one day's march from New Brunswick to Spotswood, through a region not typical of the whole of New Jersey, Quartermaster Bauer gained the following impression of the countryside: "We marched through forests the whole day. The area was poorly cultivated, and, except for a few substantial houses, there were only small huts on the new farms. In the evening we arrived at a small village named Spotswood, where we took up our quarters. There was a nice forge here."[104]

Half a year later, Quartermaster Bauer corrected his first impressions in a more general description of New Jersey: "No doubt, New Jersey is one of the most fertile and pleasant provinces in North America. There are many fine farms here, which provide everything in abundance to feed the people. But there are not enough people in this province to cultivate the land sufficiently. It could feed at least four times the number it now feeds."[105]

Another comment on New Jersey is that of Lieutenant Colonel von Dincklage of the Regiment de Corps, who said in 1778: "This province is thought to be the most fertile one in all of North America. It is mostly flat land, well cultivated and has a great number of cattle. Some parts of this province have severely suffered from the war; many houses that have been deserted by their inhabitants are burnt down and damaged. As in all provinces, cultivated land alternates with forests with all kinds of trees...."[106]

Captain Hinrichs sent quite detailed reports on Georgia and South Carolina to Baron von Jungkenn. One is titled: "A Contribution of Philosophical and Historical Remarks Concerning South Carolina,"[107] and is an appendix to his diary. However, both are much too erudite and dwell too much on the history of the two provinces not to suspect that the greater portion of both accounts is based on a painstaking study of printed sources. Hinrichs also wrote to Professor August Ludwig Schloezer in Goettingen, who published his letters from 1780 to 1787.[108] Hinrichs was much more interested in historical, political, cultural, and religious subjects than was Captain Johann Ewald, another jaeger officer.

Captain Ewald wrote the most comprehensive and voluminous diary of all Hessian officers during the war —1,137 handwritten pages in four volumes. A fifth volume with sketches and drawings, was added in 1831 by an officer of the infantry Regiment Oldenburg. Captain Ewald was a field officer with an excellent military record, who later became a Lieutenant General in the Danish service.

Ewald's diary is a most profound report on the military events of the war and can thus be considered the basic Hessian exposition of military tactics in the Revolution. Later, Ewald published a series of booklets on the "small war" [what we now call guerilla warfare]. These new tactics, which originated with the American rifleman (and adopted by Hessians, French, and English, and transferred to Europe), caused a tactical revolution in the standing armies of Euro-

SANDY HOOK LIGHT HOUSE. *This is the view seen by Lieutenant Bardeleben as the ships carrying the first Hessians to America lay at anchor for two days waiting for orders to proceed to Staten Island and debark. This aquatint in color is titled "The Light House on Sandy Hook, S.E. one Mile." Published in 1777, in ATLANTIC NEPTUNE.*

pean sovereigns. (Another young officer who was learning his craft in America during the Revolution was Cadet Neidhardt von Gneisenau, later Prussian Field Marshall-General.)

Captain Ewald's diary can be compared only with a collection of letters to Baron von Jungkenn from Major Carl Leopold Baurmeister, Adjutant General in the Hessian Corps from 1776-1784, and the diary of Captain Friedrich Ernst von Muenchhausen, Hessian wing adjutant to General Howe, or of Captain Friedrich von der Malsburg of the Regiment von Dittfurth, who wrote a noteworthy diary of the first part of the war.[109] Baurmeister and Muenchhausen give us an eyewitness report on happenings in the Hessian and English headquarters, but they leave little room for notes on the American countryside.

Rural New England got some descriptive attention. Melchior Martini, captain in the Regiment von Huyne, wrote to Baron von Jungkenn about Rhode Island: "There are only a few towns in this area but there is a farm every mile. Somebody told me that there were not more than thirty towns in America, but I have seen only New York and Newport, which are separated by a distance of about one hundred seventy English miles. Boston is about seventy miles from here; we shall probably reach it next spring on our first expedition to that area. This country has many mountains, rocks, and forests."[110]

Descriptions of Towns

American towns were favorite subjects in journals of Hessian officers. In contrast to German towns, many of which had grown around the residence of a secular or ecclesiastic prince (e.g., Cassel; Regensburg), most American towns were situated on harbors or rivers and were trading places for imported and exported raw material and manufactured goods. The Hessian officers saw these towns and described them very mechanically at first, and, later, when they got accustomed to them, more casually. These descriptions are the most impressive German testimonies of a period two hundred years past.

New York, the first city which the Hessians saw, inspired almost all diarists. One Hessian officer wrote to his brother: "To give you an impression of America, or at least of the small part of it that we are in possession of, I am about to praise it as a very pleasant and plain country, and New York is one of the most beautiful and pleasant cities that I ever saw, in spite of being burnt down towards the sea."[111] Field chaplain Kuemmel added: "New York ... is a very imposing place and one of the most elegant in America. It has many wooden houses (but most of them are built of stone), nice churches, broad streets, two German churches, one Reformed, and one Lutheran, that are now empty because of the rebellion."[112]

Lieutenant Colonel von Dincklage remarked about the city: "New York City is quite large, and thickly populated.... This place is very suitable for trade, because the biggest ships can moor on both sides of the city. Most houses are built of brick with the exception of the houses in the outskirts and the small side streets, which are built of boards and logs. There are also some nice churches and government houses. Many of them have been turned into warehouses, hospitals, and barracks."[113]

Captain Friedrich von der Malsburg of the Regiment von Dittfurth had even more praise for New York. In a detailed description of the city and its surroundings, he wrote: "I found the main streets very broad, and the most beautiful one is called 'Broadway'. But the west side of the city, toward the Hudson River, altogether nearly 1,150 houses, was turned to heaps of ashes and stone, which were still smoldering, evidence of the malice of our enemies.

"Among the buildings of worship St. Paul's Church distinguishes itself especially; it is built in Gothic style. The College Square [Kings College, later Columbia], near the Hudson River on a pleasant height, consists of a very fine building constructed also of hewn stones. It is fenced in by a high railing, which also surrounds a splendid garden and a spacious yard. This building has been donated, by voluntary contributions of the inhabitants of this province, to house and to teach a number of young students. It has a chapel, a dining hall, a library, a museum, an anatomy cabinet and a school for experimental physics. The townhall, although a massive building, does not show the taste of more recent structures. Therefore, it is less imposing than a newly built prison that stands on the large square called Common. This prison is now packed completely with rebels, who have been captured on Long and York Islands.

"The whole city is one and a half English miles long and half a mile wide.... The location of the city on the southernmost end of this island between the mouths of the North and East Rivers is undescribably pleasant, and the sight toward the harbor is very imposing. To the right the coast of New Jersey, to the left, the charming shores of Long Island, with the most beautiful farmhouses and dwellings; straight ahead, the view of Staten Island and the small islands that are scattered in the bay between here and there, such as Nutten, Governor's, Barren, and Bedlow's Island, which offer to the eye objects of pleasure and entertainment."[114]

The journal of the Hessian Corps under the command of Lieutenant General von Heister gives the following account of New York: "This city, that gave the name to the whole province,...offers a lovely sight to the sea. It has docks at different places that extend far out into the river where merchantmen dock to sell their wares without the help of a tender. Rocks line the bank to protect the nearby houses from ice when it breaks. The city is well situated for trade. It has nice broad streets, several government buildings.... churches, and many beautiful houses, most of which are built of stone, with a flat roof and a porch leading around the whole house. There are also many small houses of wood, some with only one story. There are about twenty-five hundred houses and sixteen thousand inhabitants. At this time there are probably less than one thousand, mostly women, since most of the men escaped or left with the rebels. Each craftsman has his craft's coat-of-arms with his name affixed to his house, as in England and in Cassel."[115]

Lieutenant Henkelmann wrote: "I want to tell you something about New York. It is said to have about two thousand five hundred and fifty houses, but I think that it has more than four thousand, one thousand of them burnt down when

the rebels were forced to leave the city. The following churches are in town: Three Anglican, two German Lutheran, one German Reformed, three Dutch Reformed, two English and one Scottish Presbyterian, one French, one Jewish, one Baptist, and one more, the denomination of which I have forgotten. There is also a High School, three stories high and excellently constructed but no university [in operation]. Doctors and the preachers of English language services were the only teachers, and they are now in Philadelphia, having left New York. The streets are broad and well paved....New York is said to be like Hanover. There is a fort on the seaside, constructed in a commanding way, but it is not finished yet and only armed with a few cannon, of which it should have more than two hundred...."[116]

Quartermaster Carl Bauer remarked: "New York is a big city, which is said to have had five thousand houses before the fire. Some streets are regular, others not. The city was deserted, wild, and desolate, because most inhabitants escaped because of fear. All houses were empty and most of these were turned into quarters for soldiers. New York has eighteen churches and meetinghouses, the most beautiful among them, St. Paul's and St. George's Chapel. Two of these eighteen churches were burnt down. There was also a nice college, for the present serving as a hospital for the army. A Royal shipyard is here, which cannot construct new ships but only repair old ones. The landscape around New York is very pleasant."[117]

Quartermaster Lotheisen of the Regiment de Corps gave a very different description of the city. He noted in his diary: "There is only one well for drinking water, the Tea-water Fountain. The water is leased and distributed in a cart and sold at 4-1/3 heller [118] per pail. The city has no gate but is protected by the two forts, George and Bunkershill, and by the warships at anchor."[119]

Philadelphia was also very fascinating to the Hessian observers. This city was the capital of the young nation, and the home of Congress. Due to its location on the Delaware River, the center of a densely populated area, it had grown more rapidly than other American cities, and was then the largest city in the country.

The journal of the Regiment de Corps read: "Philadelphia is the most beautiful and most regularly laid-out city in America and deserves an important rank among European cities. The city is situated on a nice plain between the Schuylkill and Delaware Rivers. At this time, it is not yet completed according to plans and only three and a half English miles long and one and a half mile wide. When we took possession of the city [September 26, 1777], it had about two or three thousand large, regular stone houses, most of them having tile roofs, contrary to other American cities, where houses have shingle roofs.

"When plans are completed, the city will spread from the Delaware River to the Schuylkill River, forming a square about five miles long and five miles wide. Both sides of the streets are paved for pedestrians like the upper town in Cassel. The main streets are wide so that three or four coaches can pass side by side. The city is so well equipped with lanterns that, when seen from the market square, it looks like a festival illumination, for all the streets are laid out squarely. The city will equal London when it is finished and will surpass it in regularity."[120]

Lieutenant von Dincklage said the following about the city: "I want to write something about Philadelphia now. The first house was built here about ninety years ago, when the whole district was nothing but forest. Now the city has already about five thousand stone houses.... There are some medium-sized and pretty churches, a beautiful townhall, some very comfortable hospitals, and a fine penitentiary.... I

VIEW OF SEVERAL PUBLIC BUILDINGS IN PHILADELPHIA. *This wood engraving shows "the beautiful townhall" mentioned by Lieutenant von Dincklage. The building is shown at center, with tower, and is now known as Independence Hall. This is a 1790 view of the Independence Hall complex published in the COLUMBIAN MAGAZINE. The text accompanying this engraving states that it shows the steeple before it had rotted so severely that it had to be torn down in 1781. The steeple was not replaced until 1828, employing a somewhat different design and outward appearance than the original. The buildings from left to right are, the Episcopal Academy, the County courthouse, Independence Hall (the State House in 1790), the Philosophical Society, the Library Company, and Carpenter's Hall. Only Independence Hall and Carpenter's Hall were in existence at the time the city was occupied by the Hessians.*

A VIEW OF NEW YORK FROM THE NORTHWEST. *This view, executed probably shortly before 1773, shows church landmarks from left to right: Trinity (on bluff), Lutheran, Middle Dutch, Wall Street Presbyterian, French Church du St. Esprit, and South Dutch. Just to left of South Dutch Church are cupola and flag of City Hall. At right, Fort and Governor's House. Published 1777, in the ATLANTIC NEPTUNE. Courtesy New York Public Library.*

have been told that at least some hundred new houses have been built each year. If it were not for this war, which not only stopped cultivation of the land but also ruined a large number of houses, the city would be almost completed. There are many airy and pretty countryhouses in the region...."[121]

Captain Hinrichs wrote about the sidewalks to Professor Schloezer in Goettingen: "A wide stone pavement in front of the houses makes walking very easy, and I must admit that this is better than in Goettingen. Here the gutters do not adjoin the sidewalk, so that the pedestrian is not forced to leave it during the rain to avoid becoming twice as wet as he would walking in the middle of the street. Each householder gets two poles in the summer, on which to fix canvass, so that one may walk in the shade."[122]

Lieutenant Ritter wrote in the journal of the Regiment von Knyphausen about Philadelphia: "The most beautiful churches are three English Episcopal churches, three Presbyterian churches, one Baptist meetinghouse, four Quaker meetings, two German Lutheran churches, one school building with towers, a new imposing Reformed church, one Methodist church, one Moravian church, two Roman Catholic churches, and a Swedish Lutheran church one mile out of town. Furthermore, there is the Academy, the townhall housing the Assembly [Independence Hall or State-House], the courthouse, the Provincial House, the penitentiary, and the barracks."[123]

The observations of Lieutenant General von Knyphausen and of Colonel von Donop differed from the other Hessian descriptions of Philadelphia. Knyphausen reported to the Landgrave regarding a letter received from Donop: "He writes that the city is well populated, but looks much more like a Dutch village and that New York must take precedence over it. I have gone there since and have found no reason to correct this opinion of Colonel von Donop."[124]

Lieutenant Colonel von Dincklage described nearby Germantown: "...the inhabitants are almost all Germans. It has one main street and nice houses built of stone; it is nearly three English miles long ....The surrounding region has many fine country houses, and this is the place where even the ladies and gentlemen from Philadelphia enjoy themselves during summertime."[125]

Major Baurmeister commented about the city of Annapolis: "In the city of Annapolis on the left shore of Maryland we saw a provincial flag, but sailed past without firing at it. This city is situated in a valley not far from the shore. With glasses we could clearly make out the streets, a big church, and other new, beautiful buildings which belong to the tobacco manufacturers—so the pilots told us. On both shores were tobacco fields, a few grain fields, large pastures with cattle, and a great deal of woods. The water in the bay at this point is fresh. The springs along the shores are clearer and colder than any in Germany."[126]

Lieutenant Piel of the Regiment von Lossberg passed through Maryland, Delaware, and Pennsylvania in 1777 as a prisoner of war after the Battle of Trenton. He described some of the towns in his diary: "We arrived at Baltimore. We were lucky to meet some French officers who became very friendly with us. Baltimore is, second to Annapolis, the most beautiful city in Maryland. It is pleasantly situated and has a good harbor on the bay. The city probably has about 600 houses, most of which are built of brick. We would have liked to spend the period of our imprisonment here, but Congress decided to send us to Dumfries in Virginia.

"Dumfries is a poor place with the exception of about forty houses, most of which are built of wood, not counting the church and the townhall. There are also many warehouses, in which tobacco is stored. The town lies on a small river, called Quantico, which flows into the Potomac about forty miles from here. In peacetime the town has had a considerable tobacco trade with England. But now trade and traffic have stopped....

"At noon [September 7, 1777] we arrived at Winchester and were quartered in several inns. This place has about 150 houses, built partly of wood, partly of stone. There is an English church here, but there has been no service for a long time. Mr. Thruston [Reverend Charles Mynn Thurston], the shepherd of this congregation, has taken up the sword. Last winter he led one hundred volunteers against the Royal Army, [at Amboy, New Jersey], got wounded, and was

awarded the rank of Colonel, with the permission to form a regiment [one of sixteen Additional regiments], which is not yet at full strength.

"The German Lutherans have erected a stone church here, which probably will not be finished for some time, because of the war and lack of money. The German Reformed church has a wooden chapel here, but no preacher. In short, religion and law have fallen asleep in America. The inhabitants are English, Scottish, Dutch, and German, the last being the most numerous. They have adopted such a mixture of language that it is difficult to understand them, no matter whether they speak English or German."[127]

Some remarks on the "Region of Williamsburg" reflected Captain Ewald's impressions: "Williamsburg is the capital of Virginia. It is situated between the Archerhop and Queen's Rivers, surrounded by hills between the springs of these two rivers. [Archerhop refers to Archers Hope, the plantation located on the west bank of College Creek near its confluence with the James River. Queen's River or Creek flows into the York River, the two streams nearly bisecting the peninsula at Williamsburg.] These hills are encircled by deep ravines that form a sort of fortified camp. Both rivers can be crossed only over two bridges near Williamsburg because of the muddy banks. This makes this region a good post for an army. But an army must also control Chesapeake Bay to avoid troops landing in its back, which we did. In this way we became masters of this excellent and beautiful area between the York and James Rivers, where a strong army can live a year."[128]

Captain Ewald described Charleston, S. C., in his usual military manner: "The city is laid out in a triangle, the long sides of which are formed by the Ashley and Cooper Rivers. It is about an hour's walk from the hornwork [tabby wall made of shells mixed with lime connecting two half-bastions above Calhoun Street between Meeting and King] to the fort which covers the harbor. At the open land side, where it is the widest, it is one quarter of an hour's walk. The streets are straight and laid out in squares. There are about 800 houses, most of them built of wood, three stories high. The number of inhabitants of all nations is said to be 6,000 whites and mulattos in peaceful times, not counting the Negroes. Most of them are merchants, living in the best taste and luxury."[129]

Quartermaster Carl Bauer gave his impressions of the same city: "Charleston could have more houses considering its area. There are numerous gardens, many of them uncultivated, vast plains leading out into the countryside. Furthermore, most of the houses are set apart, the distance between them great enough to permit fresh air to blow into the streets from all sides. To the displeasure of the pedestrians, the streets are not paved because of lack of stone. There are only narrow footpaths for the pedestrians along the houses, and even these are not everywhere. There is a gritty sand in the middle of the streets, which is whirled into the air by strong winds, causing great discomfort to the eyes. This nuisance plagues people in the houses, since they must continuously keep their windows open because of the heat."[130]

Quartermaster Kleinschmidt made reference in his journal to the churches in Charleston: "It has two English Presbyterian, one French, one German, and one Quaker, and, furthermore, a rather large townhall and theater."[131]

Lieutenant Colonel von Dincklage described the city as follows: "...the 30th I was in Charleston again and found the city more beautiful than I had imagined. The wealth of the inhabitants was apparent everywhere, even in the public buildings.... The city of Charleston is rather large, has straight streets, and many beautiful houses that are all furnished in keeping with the warm climate here. All have large rooms with windows on all sides so that the breeze can always get through. The furnishings are generally magnificent, and everything indicates a high standard of living, which is proof of the wealth of the inhabitants, who have lost a lot by this war. A large number of houses are damaged by cannon shot. Many inhabitants had erected a sort of casemate next to their houses, permitting them to live securely."[132]

Quartermaster Kleinschmidt cited in his journal, a poem written in English, which shows another face of the city:[133]

TIMOTHY FORD HOUSE. *This tasteful house is 18th century Charleston style described by the Hessians as "three stories high" and "set apart, the distance between them great enough to permit fresh air to blow into the streets from all sides." The house stands endways to the street, which is also typically Charleston. The exact date of construction of the house is not known. Timothy Ford was not in Charleston at the time of the Hessian occupation of the city. He was in Morristown, New Jersey, where at the age of sixteen, he became a friend of a young officer in General Washington's army. This officer, General Marquis de Lafayette, was a frequent visitor to the Morristown home of Timothy's mother, the widow of Colonel Jacob Ford, in whose "mansion" Washington made his headquarters during the winter of 1779-1780. The Jacob Ford home is now MORRISTOWN NATIONAL HISTORICAL PARK. In 1825, Timothy Ford entertained Lafayette in his Charleston home, pictured here. Courtesy Mr. & Mrs. A. Bert Pruitt Jr.*

A Description of Charleston, South Carolina

Whites & blacks, all mixed together, unconstant strange unwholesome weather,
Burning heat and milling cold, dangerous both to young and old.
Boisterous winds and milling rains, fever & reheumatic pains
Likewise the ague without doubt, boils, prickly heat and gout,
Many cellars full of rats, many garrets full of bats.
Mousquetous on the skin make bloches, saulupes & large cockroaches.
The water in the wells is bad, which make the inhabitants full sad,
In the streets may be seen, many whores dressed like a queen,
Some are white, some black, some yellow, some are lean, some fat and mellow,
If in your pockets you got pelf, for colour you may please yourself.
Frightful creatures in the waters, porpoises, sharks & alligators,
No lamps of light, but streets of sand, and houses built on barren land,
Markets dear and little money, large potatoes sweet as honey,
Every thing at a high price, except rum, homony and rice,
Many a widow not unwilling, and many a beau not worth a shilling,
The air is full unto my sorrow, we're here today and gone tomorrow,
No tune is play'd on the ring of bells, negroes plenty for to sell.
Parsons plenty and some poor preachures, little minded by the hearers,
In the place a number of Scotch, dram shops plenty kept by the Dutch,
No pleasure here is to be had, but getting drunk, and that is bad,
Many a bargain, if you'll strike it, this is Charleston, how do you like it?

Lieutenant Wiederholt came to a less colorful judgment. He wrote in his characteristic sharp tone: "This city is a meeting ground for all religions and nations, therefore a mixture, havens, of all sects and religious communities, not less a *confluens canaillorum'....*"[134]

Some cities inspired diarists, others did not. Of Savannah, Ga., an auditor of the Advocate General's branch of the army wrote: "Savannah, about 40 years old, lies on the 32nd degree latitude and has about 600 houses, most of them of light construction."[135] The journal of the Grenadier Battalion von Minnigerode said about the city: "...this city is not very large. The houses are only lightly constructed of wood and were severely damaged during the last siege."[136]

Captain Friedrich von der Malsburg gave a noteworthy description of Newport, R.I., and its environs: "It is situated on 41° 30' northern latitude and has 1,000 to 1,200 houses of two to three stories, most of which are built of wood and brick. There are a number of fine houses with a kind of Italian roof, which are proof of the wealth of their owners.... The city is stretched out on a hill, which begins at the seashore. It offers the inhabitants who live on top of it the most magnificent view which the eye can long for. The streets are not paved except for the most important ones. The Thames or Main Street, which runs partly along the harbor in a straight line from north to south, is half a mile long and well paved. There are few public buildings: the library, resembling a greek temple in Doric style with four pillars in front, is newly constructed of ashlars and very pretty....

"The courthouse or townhall is a large building which is constructed of brick. It stands on the parade ground and now houses the main guard.... Trinity Church, the only church of the Anglican religion, is my choice of a number of religious buildings. It still has some preachers and is filled on Sundays with a large congregation. Furthermore, there are two Presbyterian churches of good construction and appearance. But since their preachers exchanged the gun for the Bible and most members of their parish followed their example, one of these churches serves to house invalid soldiers, and the other is used for religious services of the garrison.

"The Jewish synagogue is a new, massive, and graceful building, but it is a pity that it stands in the midst of other buildings so that it cannot readily be seen. There are also in this city one Baptist, two Anabaptist, one Quaker, one Moravian Brothers church, and some other meetinghouses of sects. The harbor is safe from all winds, has room for 1,000 ships and is thought to be the best one on this continent. The shipyards extend from the middle of town down to Thames Street and to the part of the city which is called Point Bridge, close to the houses. This makes loading and unloading of goods very convenient."[137]

Remarks on the Climate

The climate of North America received considerable attention in the Hessian diaries. The extremes in temperature and humidity and the frequently rapid changes, which the Hessian soldiers experienced in the central coastal region, were something they were unaccustomed to in Germany. Many of the 4,626 Hessians who died not on the battlefield but in barracks, in hospitals, and on marches, died from illnesses directly or indirectly attributable to the weather.

The sudden change in temperature was more discomforting to the Hessian soldiers than long-lasting periods of cold. Captain Ewald recorded in his journal, at New York, in October 1780: "Since the burning southern wind [in the daytime] and the cold spells are coming again [at night], putrid fever increases among the units who have been in the south. The men die like flies, and all hospitals are filled."[138] Two years earlier, Ewald had written at Trenton in December 1776: "The weather changed rapidly with the beginning of the day—as often happens here—freezing weather followed heavy rainfall, which covered the roads with ice."[139]

Excessive heat caused heavy losses in the Hessian units, especially during the retreat of the British-Hessian Army from Philadelphia to New York. During this forced march across New Jersey in the summer of 1778 the army had to endure a heatwave, with temperatures fluctuating between 91° and 96°. Approaching Freehold, N.J., Captain Ewald wrote: "Skirmishing continued the whole time. Many men collapsed and wretchedly lost their lives because of the enormous heat, the sandy ground, and the pathless woods, with no water to be found on the whole march."[140] On June 26 the army lost about 200 men because of the heat.[141] On

June 28, the day of the Battle of Monmouth, the temperature was 96°.[142] Lieutenant von Bardeleben noted in his diary almost daily in July and August: "Very hot."[143] On June 29, 1778, Quartermaster Lotheisen wrote, at Kings Bridge: "The heat was so enormous today that almost the whole regiment was sick. When the colors arrived at the spot where we were to camp, we did not have enough men for a color guard. Many soldiers fainted that day and some of them died on the spot. We have never had greater heat during the American War."[144]

Captain Ewald noted about the climate in Virginia on August 25, 1777: "...we had a terrific thunderstorm and pouring rain. The humidity, which had been considerable during the day, increased so that one almost suffocated. This dreadful weather lasted till about 10 in the morning of the 26th. Since nobody was allowed to take along more equipment than his servant could carry on his back, we had only one shirt and a few pairs of socks,...which were wet." The following day Ewald said: "The heat was so enormous that some jaegers dropped dead. Toward evening we had some thunderstorms and a pouring rain."[145]

Later Ewald reported that there was unusual heat on New Year's Eve 1781 at Williamsburg, Va.,[146] and at the end of June 1782, at Yorktown, he commented on the climate and its effects on the soldiers: "We have had such intolerable heat for the past six weeks that many men have died of sunstroke or have lost their minds. Everything one wears feels as if it had been drawn through water because of continuous perspiration. The nights are especially dreadful when there is not enough air to breathe."[147] On September 18, 1781, the Hessian Jaeger Corps had only 29 men combat-ready. All officers of the corps were ill.[148]

View of the Countryside

When the troops of the first Hessian corps left their garrisons in Hesse in the spring of 1776, they had only vague ideas about the country in which they were to fight. German descriptions of North America were almost nonexistent, and those that did exist tended to be inaccurate and exaggerated. It was not until the Seven Years' War that some European Courts became aware of the great importance of North America. After the conclusion of the treaty of Westminster between George II and Frederic II of Prussia, Great Britain, being a coalition partner of Prussia, took over French possessions in North America. The events of this war in Europe and its extension in America, namely the French and Indian War, for the first time tied together the fate of the two continents.

Nevertheless, aside from information obtainable from translations of a few travel accounts, mainly in English and French, as well as those of Peter Kalm (translated from the Swedish and published at Goettingen, 1754-67), knowledge of North America remained quite meager for some time. The "subsidiary treaties", which sent thousands of Germans to North America, stimulated the desire of the German reading public to learn more about the New World. This demand was in a great measure satisfied by translations of travel books, and by reports of German newspapers on war events.

However, the common soldiers and many of their officers were little affected by this growing interest in America. In 1785 the Hessian Baron von der Lith reported the first impressions of Hessian troops in America, as follows: "Odd as the ideas and views of the Americans about the Hessians may have been in the beginning, so were the notions of the Hessians before their arrival, not only concerning the inhabitants but also of the country itself. They fancied that the New World had to look much different from the Old, and were surprised to see fields and forests, houses and gardens like those at home; even most animals were the same. Only in the woods, here and there, a beautifully colored bird or a snake reminded them that they were in a foreign country."[149]

The letters and diaries of Hessian officers indicated von der Lith's statement was an oversimplification. Professor August Ludwig Schloezer, of Goettingen, asked the Jaeger Captain Hinrichs to reappraise current views of North America and to correct them where necessary. Schloezer published, in the following years, many of these reports in two periodicals printed in Goettingen, a city of Hanover.[150]

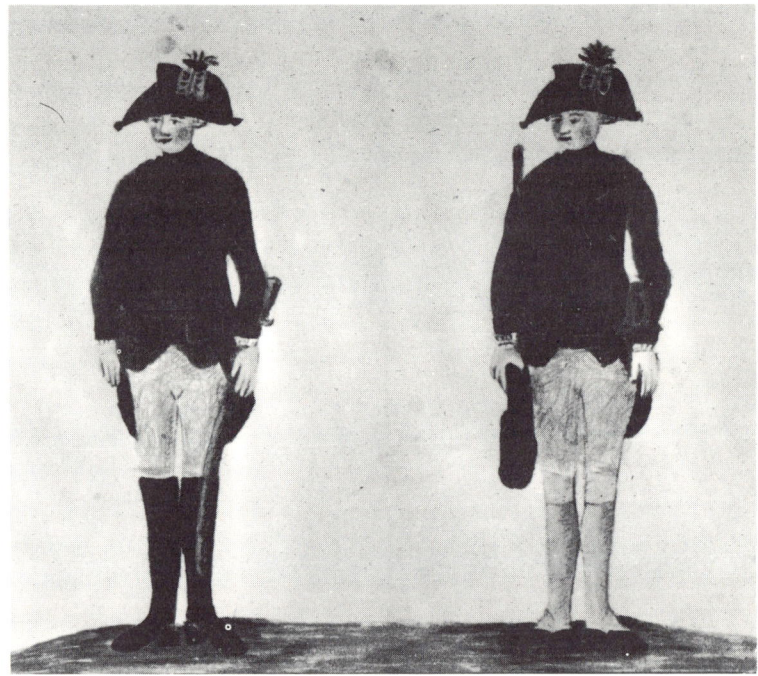

HESSIAN JAEGERS. *In 1776, the jaegers were organized into companies of foot soldiers. They were chosen for this service mainly because they were expert riflemen. The name jaeger literally means huntsman. Jaegers were recruited in Germany mainly from the ranks of gamekeepers and foresters. As the war progressed, the effectiveness of the jaegers was noted, and their numbers increased; some became mounted troops. Ultimately, the jaeger units of Hesse-Cassel, Hesse-Hanau and Anspach-Bayreuth were organized into a corps under Hessian Lieutenant Colonel Ludwig Adolph von Wurmb. Jaegers were often called "green-coats" by the Americans because of the jaeger green jackets. The trousers of their dress uniforms were yellow, but contemporary drawings and descriptions of jaegers indicate that their field uniforms called for green pants as well as jackets, undoubtedly for reasons of camouflage. The uniforms shown here are officer (left) and enlisted man (right). These sketches were made in 1786, at which time colored drawings were made of uniforms and emblems of all Hessian units. [StAM E 195/2] These sketches, when compared with earlier official Hessian Army Register word descriptions of uniforms, indicate that the 1786 sketches are reliable representations of the Hessian uniforms of 1776-83. Hessian Jaeger uniforms are described in the Army Register as follows: Coat: dark green; revers red; cuffs red; buttonholes lapeled and yellow; humeral ligament red. Waistcoat: green; sword belt red; buckle gold or yellow. Pants: yellow. Shoes or boots: black. Hat: black with green and red feather. Rifle and cartridge pouch. Knife.*

Published accounts of America were supplemented by many letter accounts. About 450 letters describing America and events of the war were written by 66 Hessian officers of all ranks, to Lieutenant General Baron von Jungkenn, Hessian Minister of State.

The reports of Captain Hinrichs are of special importance as a source of information on North America during this period. But he too was not always free of preconceived notions, prejudices, and snap judgments, as one of his letters indicated: "My previous ideas about America differ widely from those which I wrote down in my past letters in praise of North America. I still cannot imagine an earthly paradise without thinking of a large part of New Jersey and Long Island, but this is not the case with Pennsylvania. If the Honorable Count Penn would make me a present of the whole country [Pennsylvania] in exchange for my commission, under the condition that I live here the rest of my life, I would hardly accept it. And this is the praised land of milk and honey, which so many of us have lauded."[151]

Hinrichs was writing from "near Philadelphia, on The Neck" of land formed by the confluence of the Schuylkill and Delaware Rivers in the dreary month of January, and all he had seen of the Pennsylvania countryside was the stretch of land between Elk Ferry, Md., and Philadelphia, on a march which was by no means peaceful.

Notwithstanding comments such as those by Hinrichs, letters back home, in general, were welcome, even though some of the descriptions were not always true. For example in 1777, the German publisher Christian Daniel Schubarth, wrote in his *German Chronicle*: "Oh, you beloved America, you are still the hobbyhorse upon which we journalists can canter at ease. My heart jumps for joy when I hear your name. How nicely have you often helped me out of trouble! If one does not know anything, one always knows something about you! One cannot always worry about trifles, whether the reports of you are always true. Just so there is something to report! So, happily forward to America!"[152]

CHAPTER III

THE AMERICAN PEOPLE

"Rebels" and German-Americans

German views of the Revolution itself, at the beginning of hostilities in North America, differed widely. The variety of political, spiritual, and cultural life in Germany at that time, led to diverse appraisals of the events across the Atlantic. At first there seemed to be very little interest; but the course of the war and more far-reaching recruiting brought the affairs in North America more and more to the attention of the German public.

The German sovereigns who had concluded "subsidiary treaties" with Great Britain tried to influence public opinion in their territories favorable to their aims. The revolt of the Americans was represented by them from the British point of view. The Americans were portrayed as "rebels" who had risen unlawfully and arrogantly against their king. The need to support the British cause was made out to be unavoidable.

Public opinion in other German states was mostly against the "subsidiary treaties." But condemnation of the "subsidiary treaties" must not be misinterpreted; the criticism was almost exclusively directed against German sovereigns hiring out their subjects for a foreign cause. Essentially, German intellectuals were still far from approving the idea of a revolution against a legitimate sovereign.

The German officer corps in America was a part of that intellectual community back home. Their birth and education — a very large proportion belonged to the lesser nobility — did not allow any doubts about the righteousness of the British cause. Unquestionable loyalty toward their sovereign and his political and military decisions influenced their actions as well as their thinking. Quartermaster Heusser began his journal with: "When, by great insults and revolts, the inhabitants of North America forced their legitimate sovereign, King George III of Great Britain, to take up arms against them, he hired a corps of 12,000 Princely Hessian troops."[153]

Other journals voiced the same opinion. Of course, since these were the official journals, one would hardly expect disapproval of the agreements made between the British Crown and the Landgrave. Some journals, however, remained silent on the subject. To the end that there would be no adverse expressions, a representative of the Advocate General's branch of the army read an appeal of the Landgrave to the departing troops, recalling the distinction of being soldiers and reminding them of obedience to their sovereign.[154]

The disgraceful treatment of American prisoners by Hessian soldiers, during the first engagements around New York, is evidence that the Hessians really took them for "rebels" and treated them accordingly. The official journal of the Hessian corps also called the enemies "rebels".[155]

These engagements around New York exposed the Hessian troops to a new kind of war. Having been trained in linear tactics, the officers and regulars were surprised when they were forced to fight not only a regular army but also armed civilians. Accustomed to outmaneuver the enemy, cannonade and overrun him on the battlefield, they had to develop new tactics against an enemy who suddenly appeared, attacked, and retreated wherever he could. Hessian remarks of that time showed contempt for the enemy because of such tactics.

Lieutenant Schotten of the Regiment von Mirbach noted in his diary about the Battle of Long Island: "Meanwhile some men of our field picket, which had to cover our camp, had captured, at dawn, in a grainfield, a rebel general. They immediately robbed him [Brigadier General John Sullivan] of his belongings and treated him so roughly that he complained to General Heister.... This night several rebels dared to attack our outposts. They withdrew after some rounds of platoon fire, which was new to them."[156] Some time later Lieutenant Colonel von Dincklage wrote: "...today we cut the aiguillettes from our uniforms and the stripes from our hats. This was ordered so that we could not be distinguished from the common soldiers."[157]

Other reports on early engagements on Long Island follow: Captain Friedrich von der Malsburg— "The outposts of the rebels often tried to talk to ours and to invite them to their homes. But since everything is answered with silence, they take revenge for this insult by scolding and abusive language."[158]

Lieutenant Rueffer— "The enemy are hidden behind thick bushes, and we would not have known of their presence if they had not fired at us. They were all so fearful that they almost preferred to get shot rather than accept our pardon, for their generals and officers had told them that we would hang them."[159]

Colonel Johann August von Loos, in September 1776—"If they are all as bad as they were today, this will be more like a hunt than a war. But many brave boys can be killed by these rascals, and that would be a shame...."[160]

About a year later, von Loos, like many other Hessian officers, thought differently of American soldiers: "I am compelled to lay aside the Hessian prejudices that the rebels are not brave soldiers. Our losses prove that we were wrong....and if they had better officers...our job would be much tougher...."[161]

It did not take long before the first friendly contacts between Hessian soldiers and captured Americans were made. Captain von der Malsburg described one such occasion after the capture of Fort Washington in November 1776: "I met a number of captive enemy officers, in whose faces I saw fear because of the uncertainty of their treatment. They invited me into their huts and offered me punch, wine, and cold food, which I first refused but later accepted because they insisted. They seemed to be surprised by the affability of a Hessian officer, as they called it, and told me this was contrary to the descriptions they had been given...."[162]

Scorched Earth and Spies

The American concept of surprise attacks and the scorched earth policy made considerable impression on the Hessian officers. Lieutenant von Bardeleben wrote following the first encounter with American forces on Long Island in 1776: "Everywhere on this march we found signs of enemy anger which they had left on this island during their flight at our first landing. Burned houses, the grain in the fields partly in ashes, the roads spread with dead cattle. Here and there some old people, sadly looking at their homes which had gone up in flames and which still revealed a luxurious splendor, as though in paradise....Everywhere were chests of drawers, chairs, mirrors, gilt frames, porcelain in abundance, all gracefully manufactured. It was sad to see this and much more being destroyed and scattered around."[163]

Captain of Engineers Reinhard Jacob Martin noted in Philadelphia in 1778: "...There were empty houses everywhere; this proves that Congress' orders to leave the houses at our approach was true. But they did not have sufficient time to drive away their cattle."[164] Another officer reported from Savannah, Ga., in 1779: "the inhabitants had buried most of their belongings or else carried them into the country. The finest furniture, tables, and chairs of mahogany were dashed to pieces and scattered in the streets; it was a dreadful sight!"[165]

Armed civilians and their intelligence activities caused the Hessians special trouble. It must have been militiamen who were referred to in the journal of Regiment von Knyphausen in December 1776 at Trenton, N.J.: "A party of farmers with rifles attacked the wagons and burned some of them."[166] The journal of the Jaeger Corps reported, also from Trenton, that civilians often assembled to attack English depots and ammunition dumps. The writer continued: "It is almost impossible to attack the enemy at any time by surprise because each house which we pass is more or less a lookout. The farmer, his son, or the farmhand either fire a rifle or run along a footpath to inform the enemy."[167]

Captain Ewald reported that American women smuggled provisions and equipment underneath their clothes through the Hessian lines,[168] and he warned his men about talking to civilians. Ewald said: "This is especially necessary in enemy country, where everybody is against you and tells a lie to bring the enemy upon you."[169] Ewald continued: "You never get correct information about the enemy. Each step is betrayed at once and you are soon surrounded from all sides by armed civilians, not a part of the regular army of the enemy, and they all are very good marksmen."[170] Ewald ended his statements on this subject with the remark: "One can easily see how difficult reconnoitering can be in this war, because all inhabitants are spies or soldiers."[171]

The American attack on Trenton on December 26, 1776, which caught the Hessian garrison by surprise, is a good example. The complete victory of Washington here was due mostly to the fact that the Hessian commander in chief at Trenton, Colonel Rall, was unable to reconnoiter the country with any degree of security.

American spies planned and carried out sabotage or collected information on the enemy army by various methods, often camouflaged as traders in an enemy garrison.[172] Although spies faced the death sentence, this did not seem to be a deterrent; but was suffered with so much pride and courage that Hessian officers were highly impressed. Quartermaster Carl Bauer reported on the execution in New Brunswick, N.J., of an American captain who had been sentenced to death for spying: "The enthusiasm of this spy was so great that, upon reaching the ladder, he climbed it calmly, pulled the white cap over his eyes, and said to the people standing around: 'I die for freedom!'"[173]

Civilian spies traveled around in neutral areas, claimed to be English or Hessian stragglers, asked for directions, and then arrested those who helped them.[174] Captain Martin of the engineers wrote: "With stern severity, Congress forces the taking of an oath by which all inhabitants formally renounce their obedience to the King and Parliament, and cruel punishment is meted out to those who refuse to take this oath. To escape these cruelties, the Loyalists had to flee, leaving behind all their possessions. Most of them went to New York, which place many of those unfortunate Virginia families also reached."[175]

Treatment of Loyalists

The fate of the Loyalists who did not escape to safer territory is described by Captain von der Malsburg as the British and Hessians were retreating from recently occupied ground: "On our march yesterday we could clearly see the different views of the inhabitants of both sexes. The few who still were loyal to the King and had taken an oath looked sadly after us and were frightened to be again exposed to being maltreated by their wrathful fellow citizens. The others did not seem to be much worried and could hardly suppress their joy at our retreat....

"Today the rebels followed us with a strong corps and burned down the houses of all inhabitants who had sworn allegiance to the King. The largest part of the hamlet of Terrytown [Tarrytown, N.Y.] which was several miles in front of our lines had this cruel fate. We saw the flames,

REGIMENT VON KNYPHAUSEN. *This regiment was part of the nearly thousand-man, three-regiment brigade captured at Trenton on December 26, 1776. After the battle, 868 rank and file of the brigade were taken to the Pennsylvania-Dutch country of Pennsylvania. The few escapees from this brigade were temporarily placed in one unit, called The Combined Battalion. By September 1779, sufficient recruits had arrived from Germany so that the von Knyphausen regiment could be re-established. Soon thereafter, on September 9, 1779, the von Knyphausen regiment embarked as a part of a twenty-two transport fleet bound for Canada. Four days out of New York, a storm hit the fleet and two of the ships carrying the von Knyphausen regiment became disabled and were captured by the Americans and taken to the port of Egg Harbor, New Jersey. From here the captured von Knyphausen regiment was moved to Reading, Pennsylvania, in the same general area where the first Knyphausen contingent had been taken. Pictured here are the 1786 sketches of officer and enlisted man uniforms. [St AM E/195/2] Following is the earlier Hessian Army Register word description of the uniforms: Coat: dark blue; revers blue; cuffs black; buttonholes lapeled and white; humeral ligament white. Waistcoat: yellow; sword belt white; buckle gold or yellow. Pants: white. Shoes or boots: black. Helmet: copper with yellow drapery. Hat: black with yellow drapery. Rifle and cartridge pouch. Sword.*

deplored the miserable ones, and had again become convinced of the cruel behavior of our enemies toward their brothers who had different views."[176]

The Loyalists of North America could have played a more important role in the Revolutionary War if the British had made better use of them. At the beginning of the war, it is reported, about one third of the white population in the North American colonies was loyal to the Crown. During the war their number declined steadily.

During the British advance through New Jersey in December 1776, Captain Ewald wrote: "The news that Washington had not more than 8,000 men and that many of them deserted every day, reached us during the march, especially in the region of Hackensack, where we found many Loyalists. There also arrived several distinguished men from Pennsylvania who urgently requested General Howe to attack General Washington as forcefully as possible.... Some of these men, especially Mr. [Joseph] Galloway, became so angry about the delay of the British that he shouted that it was obvious they did not want to finish the war. Everyone of sound judgment was inclined to have the same thoughts."[177]

The retreat of the British-Hessian army from Philadelphia to New York in the summer of 1778 caused many Loyalists to go over to the side of Congress, for Loyalists as well as "Rebels" were plundered by the retreating troops. Major Baurmeister of the Hessian Headquarters reported at that time: "Although the men were never in need of salt or fresh provisions, there was much plundering, which disturbed General Clinton. There is much new evidence of it in Jersey. It has made the country people all the more embittered rebels. There was no pillaging and plundering on the part of the Hessians, but it is my duty to report to Your Lordship that we had many deserters."[178] Notes of Captain Ewald showed that British strategy, in general, tolerated only loyalty to the King. However, British power did not reach much further than did British guns.[179]

The following account of Ewald sheds a softer light on this question. In South Carolina he met a farmer of whom he asked directions to Charleston and learned that this man's son was a major in the Continental Army: "I intended to send this good man to Lord Cornwallis, but since his wife implored me with tears in her eyes, I did not do it and reported his statements personally. I asked the man why he had given his son into the service of the 'rebels' and not into the service of the King. The man replied, 'During the whole war we have been under orders of Congress, and there was not the least help from the King's side which the well-disposed subjects, whose number was not small, could have depended upon. Last year a very small army under the British General Prevost appeared here but pillaged friend and enemy.

"'After having accepted their protection against the exhortions of Congress, General Prevost had to retreat hastily because of the superior army of General Lincoln. My son was not in uniform at that time, but as soon as the English had left our region, I had the choice either to give my son into the service of his country or to leave my whole property. Now, Sir, look at my house; everything is my own as far as you can see. This honest wife is my own, and I have five more children in the house. Can you still blame my decision?' I shrugged my shoulders, agreed with him in my heart, esteemed the uprightness of this man, and let him peacefully return to his home."[180] And in 1781, after Yorktown, when the English and Hessian troops left Portsmouth and Gloucester in Virginia, Ewald asked: "What will be the fate of the Loyalist inhabitants there? Haven't we turned them into unhappy people?"[181]

When British bases, such as New York, were evacuated after the armistice, many Loyalists left the United States and emigrated to Canada, Nova Scotia, and the West Indies, where land was granted to them.[182] Ewald commented on this exodus in the following words: "It is a touching sight to see so many upright friends of the King moving to areas of wilderness. Most of them lived honestly in this country, and now they must start anew as their forefathers did.... Is it God's wish to ignore these poor people who have sacrificed everything for their mother country?"[183]

The opinions of the Hessians concerning German-Americans are of special interest. Throughout the war German-Americans sided with Congress almost without exception. Especially, the German-Americans of Pennsylvania, Maryland,

and Virginia became ardent supporters of the Revolution. Their total number (male, female, and children) in the year 1776 was about 200,000.

During the first months of the war, many German-born settlers and Americans of German descent were enlisted in the American army. In May 1776, Congress decided to recruit a regiment exclusively of Germans from Pennsylvania and Maryland.[184] In Pennsylvania, the Germans formed organizations, whose committees accelerated the recruiting for the American forces by public meetings, printing and distributing pamphlets, and collecting arms. Cavalry detachments from Pennsylvania and some high-ranking officers of German descent rendered outstanding service in the Army.

Most of the statements of Hessian officers regarding the German-Americans were critical. The principal reason for this attitude was the officers' social and economic background, which sheltered them from knowing of the poverty that drove their less fortunate countrymen to seek a new life across the Atlantic.

Another reason for the critical attitude of the Hessian officers may have been the very concept of revolution. They learned that the overwhelming part of the German-Americans fought for the cause of independence and used every opportunity to make this clear. This, they could not understand. A Hessian officer who was captured at Trenton reported that the German-born field-chaplains of the American Army "wretchedly insulted the King of England" and tried to "convert" everybody.[185]

Captain von der Malsburg reported after the first engagement on Long Island in August 1776: "We are more and more convinced of the disorder and lack of discipline among our enemies.

"They insult and berate us with the vilest words. As disciplined soldiers we disregard this undisciplined behavior with silence and contempt. There are many Germans among them, who especially distinguish themselves in this insolence. They shouted out their insulting words [in German] so loudly last night that we were disturbed during our encampment."[186]

An experience of Captain Ewald in Maryland showed the behavior of many German-Americans toward the Hessian troops and, at the same time, helps to explain the background of this peculiar relationship. Ewald said: "This region is well cultivated, the inhabitants are mostly Germans, but have a very bad opinion of us. They could hardly hide their anger and their hostile thoughts. An old woman, sitting on a bench in front of a house, answered in a true Palatinate dialect when I rode up to her and asked for a glass of water, 'I shall give you water, but I must also ask you, what harm have we done to you. You Germans come here to ruin us and to chase us from our homes. We have heard enough of your plundering; you will do the same here as you did in New York and New Jersey, but you will be punished for it.'"[187]

In personal contact, the relationship between Hessians and German-Americans often surmounted the barrier of political enmity. Captain Hinrichs reported from Philadelphia: "As far as I can tell, I like it here. My host is a determined rebel from Nuremberg. He contends that I should stay in Philadelphia and in his arguments he misses none of the details when he talks about the despotism of the King."[188]

Lieutenant Wiederholt, the most chauvinistic of the Hessian diarists, commented in a harsh tone on the Germans in Pennsylvania: "Most inhabitants of German descent are of

CORNWALL, PENNSYLVANIA IRON WORKS. *When 868 rank and file Hessian soldiers were taken prisoners at Trenton, it was soon found that very few of these enlisted men could speak English. They were therefore hustled off to the Pennsylvania-Dutch country where the majority of the inhabitants spoke German. (The officers were sent to Virginia.) After a short time in detention camps, 397 of these rank and file prisoners were farmed-out to local farmers and artisans. Standard pay to each farmed-out prisoner was, "in addition to food and drink, one shilling in Virginia money, thirty-five of which make one guinea." The largest contingent that went to one person was 12. These men were employed by Colonel Curtiss Grubb of the Cornwall Iron Works. Colonel Grubb had "asked for some prisoners from Lancaster" and the first to be alloted to him were eight men from the Hessian artillery. This furnace was being employed by the young United States to make cannon for the army, and the first cannon was delivered October 26, 1776, but most of the early output was not up to requirements. Soon after the Hessian artillery men came to the works, between September 16 and November 20, 1777, the quality of cannon produced at Cornwall improved. In total, 42 cannon were made at this works during the war. Pictured here is one of the cannon (an early reject), which never left the works. It now stands on the very same casting floor at Cornwall where it was made nearly 200 years ago. Courtesy the Pennsylvania Historical Museum Commission.*

the lowest class and are the dregs of that nation. They want to imitate the hospitality and candor of the others, but they remain raw and unrefined German peasants. They are steeped in the American idea of Liberty but know nothing of what liberty really is and are therefore worse than all others and almost unbearable. But here and there one finds honest and upright Germans."[189]

These testimonies show us that the revolutionary spirit of the German-Americans and their struggle for liberty were dominant factors preventing the Hessian officers from sympathetic contact with their fellow countrymen. If we had a reasonable sampling of diaries and correspondence of the rank and file Hessians, the picture might be quite different. Much of the desertion, especially during the last years of the war, was the result of the rank and file having become acquainted with German-Americans and their way of life.

Negroes and Indians

Hessian reports from North America contained numerous observations on Negroes and Indians. The first Hessian commander in chief, Lieutenant General Leopold von Heister, mentioned the black slaves in a report to the Landgrave in the winter of 1776. He found the sale of a Negro of particular interest. He did not neglect to inform the Landgrave that a Negro would gain his freedom the very moment when he should arrive in Great Britain.[190]

At the beginning of the war, and again toward the end of it, some Hessian officers sent young Negroes to Germany. Colonel Carl von Donop sent a thirteen-year-old Negro back home. Field-chaplain Koester of von Donop's Regiment taught the boy German and gave him instruction in the Christian religion before departing.[191]

The Minister of State, von Jungkenn, mentioned in a letter to Captain Friedrich von Eschwege that a Negro, named Seimsen, was still a drummer in a battalion in Cassel, and that he did not like it too much in that part of the world, and since he was no longer a prisoner, he was to be discharged so that he could go back to America. But von Jungkenn hoped that he could be made to change his mind.[192] Captain Johann Jacob Fischer of the Regiment Prince Carl sent a young Negro from Virginia to Hesse with Captain Krug to serve as drummer with the 1st Battalion of the Guards. Von Jungkenn said the boy arrived in Cassel in May 1783.[193]

In order to weaken the American forces, the British commander in chief, General Clinton, while in North Carolina, during 1779, urged the Negroes to come over to the British Army. Further, he ordered that all Negroes who joined the American Army would be punished if caught.[194] This proclamation attracted many blacks into British camps, so that feeding them raised serious problems. The train of Negroes grew from day to day and the ratio between fighting troops and non-combatants became steadily worse.

Captain Ewald wrote a vivid description of this train in North Carolina in 1780/81: "I cannot deny that the enormous train of the army astonished me considerably. Not being accustomed to it as yet, the army looked to me like a migrating Arabian or Tartar horde. Since the army had fought continuously during the last ten months in the country, Lord Cornwallis had agreed that the company officers could keep two horses and one Negro....

"But since there was no strict control, this arrangement got out of hand, and the corps of Sir William Phillips, which I had left less than three months ago, adopted a new practice, as had also the jaeger detachment and the Rangers. Each officer had four or six horses, three to four Negroes and sometimes one or two Negresses as cook or mistress. Each soldier's female companion was on horseback and had one more Negro and Negress, also on horseback, as servants. Each corporal's guard had one or two horses and Negroes and each corporal had two horses and a Negro. Indeed, I can say that each soldier had his Negro to carry his food and his bundle.

"This disorderly train was followed by about 4,000 more Negroes of every age and sex. The regions through which this train passed were eaten barren, like a field that has been attacked by a swarm of locusts. I don't know what these people lived on. It was fortunate that the army seldom stopped longer than one day or one night. When I arrived at the jaeger detachment, I found more than twenty horses and almost each jaeger had his Negro, which I corrected within twenty-four hours.

"What made this unusual, large train look so unmilitary was the varicolored clothing of these black people.... They had plundered wardrobes of their masters, distributed the clothing among themselves, and partly dressed themselves with their loot.... A near naked Negro, for instance, wore a pair of silk trousers, another a fine colored coat, the third a silk waistcoat without sleeves, the fourth a fine shirt, the fifth a fine castor hat, and the sixth a wig; the others were naked. One Negress wore a silk skirt, the other one a loincloth with a long train, the third a cape, the fourth a silk corset, the fifth a silk bodice, the sixth, seventh, eighth and ninth several different sorts of hats and wigs.

"Imagine these multicolored creatures on horseback in the thousands, and you have the whole scene. When I first saw this train, I was at my wit's end, and I wondered about the easy-going nature of Lord Cornwallis, much as I admired him for his military abilities, and I longed to be able to paint a picture of the scene."[195]

These poor people who thought by changing their clothes they could change their lives, were soon to be disillusioned. The British High Command considered the captured Negroes to be chattel that could be disposed of like any other object.[196] Only a few of them were put to proper use in the British Army. Captain Ewald used them as mounted scouts and lookouts.[197]

When the number of Negroes in the train of the army became a serious burden to warfare, the British High Command got rid of them in the same thoughtless manner as it had earlier raised their hopes for freedom and humane treatment. Shortly before the siege of Yorktown, in the late fall of 1781, the Negroes were chased away from the train of the army. Captain Ewald reported at that time: "I almost forgot to report a cruelty. On the same day that we were attacked by the enemy, all our black friends, who had been freed and dragged away to prevent them from working in the fields, and who also served very well in making entrenchments, were chased towards the enemy. They trembled at having to go back to their former owners. I had to make a secret patrol last night and met many of these unhappy ones, who were desperate because of hunger and who sought help because they were between the two firing lines. This act of cruelty became necessary because of lack of food, but one should have thought earlier to save them."[198]

After the war, all Negroes under British control were given back to their former masters under article six of the preliminary peace treaty between Great Britain and the United States. Captain Ewald commented on this article as follows: "It is also irresponsible relative to Negroes. An order was published in the name of the King, that all Negroes who had served as slaves of the rebels and who left their masters should be free; and now these innocent creatures are left to the mercy of their former masters. Is this not an affront to all rights of mankind?"[199]

None of the Hessian officers wrote concerning the origins and background of slavery in North America. They simply reported what they saw, and their comments were natural expressions of human understanding and feeling.

Quartermaster Carl Bauer, while in South Carolina during the year 1780, wrote: "I have never seen the whites doing any labor. Everything is done by Negroes, who are found in all houses in great numbers. Those who serve their masters in the city and in the country as attendants, are well kept. The fate of the field Negroes on the plantations is much harder and inhuman. The former either live with their master in his house, or have a nearby house to live in. The latter, who till the soil, are often treated worse than an ox in Europe. They walk naked and can hardly cover their chastity with an old rag. Miserable huts of logs, piled one upon another, with neither fireplace nor hearth are their living quarters.

"Their cooking equipment usually consists of a big iron pot. Sometimes I have seen no more than a bucket in the hut. As his food, the Negro gets daily one quart of corn or rice. The corn is rough-ground in a handmill outside of the hut. At the fireside in the middle of the hut is the iron pot, in which the ground corn or the rice is prepared. As soon as it has swelled, it is eaten, so as to add bulk. This is the whole food except water. The bed of these miserable creatures is the ashes around the fire. There are four or five hundred or more of these poor human creatures on some plantations, their number having no relation to the size of the plantation.

"They have to cultivate fields naked in the greatest heat. Punishment is barbaric and contrary to human principles. For simple disobedience they are pulled up with their hands tied together and flogged most cruelly on the naked back....If the master kills a slave, nobody makes a great stir about it. When a Negro strikes a white person or only raises his hand against him, he must die.... Among themselves they speak mostly the Guinean language. Most field Negroes do not understand English. A Negro can earn for his master about 500 pounds a year with the cultivation of indigo, as I was told."[200]

Carl Bauer's indignation was shared by other Hessian officers. With his sword, Lieutenant Colonel von Dincklage stopped some citizens in Charleston from flogging a Negro to death because he had called them 'rebels' and had tried to go over to the British forces. Von Dincklage commented: "What kind of a stubborn creature can man be, I thought as I went off. Those who only talk and write about freedom and who try to prove by every kind of argument that all human beings are born free, are the same ones who treat their fellow-men most terribly and do not grant a shadow of freedom to those who are in their power."[201]

Lieutenant Wiederholt made some general comments on the Negroes and stated the opinion of most Hessian observers on this subject: "The law of nature should teach each despot to handle even the lowest slave humanely, for they are human beings of the same kind as he is and we all are, in spite of the fact that fate did not make them masters but slaves when they were born.

"I must make another remark on the Negroes that shows how they are treated, how blindly they are led and that they are kept away from all knowledge of God and His Word to make them believe that they are of a lower race of men than we are, meant only to be slaves.... The blacks have a sensitive part by nature and nobody can deny that they have a better character than the whites in spite of the fact that their appearance does not portray this.

"The bad treatment in respect to all the necessities of life, and the knowledge that they are slaves and of a low position makes them all quiet and sad. The barbaric treatment they get from some is a disgrace to all mankind, and being a witness to it horrifies me. The Americans have no such feelings despite claiming to be sensitive and hospitable."[202]

Hessian contact with Indians occurred on a different basis. In the first engagement between Hessians and Indians, the latter were completely annihilated.[203] In the course of the following years the British High Command managed to win many Indians to its side. The continuous struggle of the Indian tribes to defend their hunting grounds against white American settlers, eased the task of the British. But the alliance with some Indian tribes in the year 1777 was of doubtful value to the British Crown.

The Indians proved to be unreliable allies who did not know discipline and coordination in warfare. After a battle, they would continue to fight,[204] and would scalp everyone in sight, even many Loyalists and neutral Americans. Since the use of Indians by the British stiffened American resistance, this practice seems to have been of no special advantage to the English Command.[205] Therefore, they were later used only as scouts.

They were not dependable in the heat of battle, and gave up quickly if they did not find rich booty. Sometimes they broke their treaties of alliance with the British, if it was to their advantage. When General Bourgoyne had heavy losses during the battles near Bennington and Fort Stanwix in the fall 1777, the Indians abrogated the pact of alliance after the engagement at Stillwater, and retreated, looting and burning on their way back to their home territory.

The Indian chiefs who appeared at headquarters appeared colorful, even to the brightly uniformed soldiers, and were the object of detailed Hessian descriptions. Captain Ewald described a chief of the Lower-Creek Indian tribe near Charleston, S.C.: "The Indian commander was known by the name 'Raving Wolf'. He was a great warrior who had never lived in peace with the neighboring nations. He was of a copper color and of medium size, his eyes sparkled like fire, and his dress was as follows: He wore a shirt of raw linen which was over a blue coat with red facings and collar, and he wore neither trousers nor stockings. His feet were covered with sandals. His head was shaved up to the crown, and from his ears, which were pierced, hung pendants of silver. He carried pistols and swords. His face was here and there painted red, and he wore a double silver ring in his nose. He had skillfully bound a silk cloth around his head that was fastened with silver clasps. He wore a silver collar at his chest and silver bracelets around his arms (tied with red ribbons),

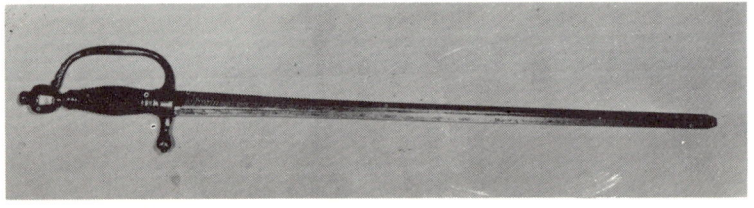

HESSIAN OFFICER'S SWORD. *The blade of this sword is etched "Friedrich, II Landgraf zu Hessen." Courtesy National Park Service, Morristown National Historical Park.*

which were a present from England with 'George Rex' engraved on them."[206]

Captain Hinrichs said of the southern tribes, the Upper- and Lower-Creeks, Chickasaw, and Cherokee, that they were not as uncultured as commonly claimed, because they had their belief in honor, religion, friendship and revenge.[207]

Habits and Religions

Despite the fact that Hessian troops stayed over seven years in North America, there were surprisingly few reports on American customs. Perhaps they did not find them to be very different from those of Germany. However, some diarists did describe homes they visited and, by implication, some aspects of the American way of life.

Hessian observers were impressed by the layout and furnishings of American homes. Some of their accounts missed no details. The following description of one of the homes of Newport, R.I., is taken from the diary of Captain von der Malsburg: "The interior is comfortably furnished. Adjoining the entrance hall there usually are the rooms which are called parlor (the master's living room), dining room, and drawing room (room for visitors). The living rooms of the family and the bedrooms are upstairs. The kitchen is in the back part of the ground floor. The quarters for the slaves, the coach houses, and stables are in the yard. Here, too, or in the garden at the greatest distance from the house, are the very neatly built privies. The houses of the rich also have a yard in front, which is enclosed with an iron fence. The furniture is made of mahogany, and in the homes of the rich, of even more costly wood, all expertly manufactured.

"All the floors are covered with carpets of the most lively colors, and all rooms have sofas. Wallpaper, except for some made of genuine Indian-print cotton, is but little used. In its place they have paneling from floor to ceiling, which, painted a silver color and often hung with beautiful paintings, gives the rooms a friendly and lived-in appearance. In the middle of the wall, opposite the door, there is usually a fireplace, the utensils of which are of neatly polished iron, mounted with the finest brass and in some houses even with silver. Above the fireplace is the mantlepiece, which is adorned with clocks or bronze figures. Behind it and at both sides there are mirrors. The side mirrors are crowned with large candelabra. Next to these, on both sides, are what might be called cupboards, the bottom parts of which are used for storage of wood, the top sections serving as sideboards.

"To enter such a drawing room on a winter evening affords a pleasant sight, largely because of the fire in the fireplace, which is kept going with neatly hewn logs, and because of the shining utensils. The fireplaces are lined on the inside with black marble or similar material [possibly slate] and have a marble plate in front, about one foot wide, which is framed by a nicely pierced steel or brass skirt to prevent the scattering of coals. When there are coals or ashes in this space, the master of the house, or anyone else who cares to, immediately sweeps it back into the fire with a small broom, the fire being kept going continuously.

"The whole family gathers around the fireplace and is always prepared to see friends and relatives. In smaller houses everything is plainer but no less appropriate. The doors of the wealthy are locked, but as soon as the knocker is heard, it is

THE HUNTER HOUSE. *This probably is the Newport house described by Captain von der Malsburg. It is early New England Georgian in design. It was constructed about 1748, and is in THE NATIONAL REGISTER OF HISTORIC PLACES. It is located at 54 Washington Street, Newport, R. I., and is owned and shown by the Preservation Society of Newport County.*

opened by a slave. Cleanliness, this unmistakable sign of wealth, is visible everywhere, even to certain extremes, and it keeps the slaves busy enough."[208]

Von der Malsburg gave a detailed description of the eating habits of residents of New Jersey. He wrote: "Their manners are simple and orderly, without drinking bouts and orgies. Their lunch consists mostly of a piece of salted beef or pork, potatoes, green lettuce, salt-water fish and oysters, which are plentiful here, dried rusk, or a sort of cake made of corn and wheat flour. This is made daily or even for each meal. It is a substitute for bread, which is almost unknown here. The sort of bread that can be seen here is sold to our soldiers and is baked of wheat flour. Brown and sour-dough bread is completely unknown here. Cyder or grog are common drinks for the common man at each meal. The more wealthy drink Madeira, Port, and other good wines, and they also have better food. They do not drink much coffee; tea is their favorite drink and is drunk several times a day. Butter and cheese are served with it."[209]

Quartermaster Kleinschmidt added some further remarks: "At dinner parties they have completely adopted the English manners. All dishes appear at the same time, everybody eats and drinks as much as he wishes and what he wishes. They do not offer a second helping; you must ask for it. They do not serve much soup, but there are four or five vegetables, and boiled potatoes are served at each meal. They drink punch, cider, strong and port beer, grog (rum mixed with water), Madeira, Port, Claret, Sherry, Lisbon and Tyal wine, toddy (a drink consisting of a mixture of rum, water, sugar and nutmeg), sugarie (wine, water, and sugar), silabub (Madeira wine, sugar and milk). All these drinks are hot, but they are accustomed to them that way. They do not drink much at dinner.

"Usually two sit together and drink after the meal. One asks another to drink a glass of wine with him, and it would be considered an insult if you refuse. After the dinner, when everything has been taken from the table, even the tablecloth, different wines are served and toasts are given. The bottles begin with the master of the house, and go around the table to the left. Each one passes the bottles to his neighbor so he can chose the variety of wine he wants. The toasts go around to the right."[210]

Lieutenant Wiederholt, always striking a more critical tone than do his fellow officers, wrote about American cooking: "I do not like their cooking of vegetables and dinners. They always serve meat with a few bad and half-boiled vegetables. These are their meals, and their beverages are grog or toddy. Grog is water and rum, toddy is the same, but some sugar and toasted crust of white bread are added. It is a good drink in summer because it satisfies one's thirst without harm even if you take a big sip in the heat."[211]

Lieutenant Henkelmann described the day of the average middle-class American family: "When they get up they drink tea and eat a plate full of sandwiches. About noon or one o'clock in the afternoon they roast either beef or pork on the coal fire; then eat, and drink tea; they do the same in the evening, and so the day passes. The women do nothing except wait for tea time, pretty up the rooms, and sit at the fireplace. Stoves are not common here in spite of the fact that there is enough iron. At home we could have a fire for a week, using the amount of wood which is here burnt in twenty-four hours. The fat that runs into the fire here would make a nice soup at home."[212]

Captain von der Malsburg described the clothing of Americans: "The dress of the men and their sons (I talk of the lower class) is very light and easy and consists of a short, striped linen jacket; the knickers, called 'trousers', reach down to the heel. You do not see anything tied or buckled on the whole body. Therefore, growth is not hindered and straight bones and high statures are the result. The female sex is better dressed. Women dress like the well-to-do middleclass German woman. On their heads they wear a black hat or bonnet of damask, bombace, or silk. Young girls wear nothing on their heads; their hair is done like that of our ladies, in a fold, with the chignon hanging down."[213]

Lieutenant Henkelmann wrote his impressions of the American woman to Minister of State von Jungkenn: "As blessed as this continent may be, as proud and lazy are its owners. A lady has nothing to do but dine and drink, adorn herself, drive about, and sleep."[214]

The following are notes of Lieutenant Colonel von Dincklage about the inhabitants of Pennsylvania: "It is obvious that the customs here are not the best. First, because of the marked personal freedom to act and to live as one wants to, and second, because the immigrants from all parts of the world have brought with them not only good habits but also bad ones. The tendency to self-indulgence and luxury, especially among women, is wholy unrestrained."[215]

American Religious Life

The Hessian observers never failed to name the kind and number of churches when they described an American town. This suggests that the writers were surprised by the variety of religious communities in North America. They noted especially the coexistence of different religions and sects, for this was not yet common in Germany, where their forefathers had experienced bitter religious wars, which split the unity of the German Empire for almost two centuries.

While most of the Hessian officers rejected the idea of revolution as a matter of principle, they appear to have admired the freedom of American religious life. The journal of the Regiment von Huyne, written by Quartermaster Kleinschmidt, expressed this feeling: "They tolerate all religions here, and the government even allows them to celebrate their services in public."[216] Kleinschmidt further described one of these public events in Providence, R.I.: "The Freemasons today celebrated St. John's Day and proceeded in their gowns accompanied by two bands of musicians through the city and into the church."[217]

The religious sect that drew more attention than any other were the Quakers, partly because their religious tenets did not permit them to take an active part in the war. Quakers frequently treated Hessian casualties. Hessian stories about their way of life are therefore numerous.

Quartermaster Kleinschmidt wrote: "The Quakers, of whom there are many here [Providence, R.I.], can be easily distinguished from the other inhabitants, not only because of their simple clothes, but also because they do not like praise and acclaim. They like neither music nor dancing. When with others, they are very modest and do not talk much. When they officiate at divine service, everybody who is inclined to, or, as they call it, 'moved by God's spirit', may preach, be it man or woman. They do not have hymn books and therefore do not sing but sit quietly."[218]

Kleinschmidt took part in a Quaker wedding, together with some other Hessian officers, and reported: "On the 29th I attended a Quaker wedding, which was held without ceremonies as follows: After sitting quietly for more than one hour, having heard a poorly delivered and short sermon by an old woman, the bride and bridegroom stood up and shook hands. Then the bridegroom said as follows:

'This (name to be named) is the person whom I
'Hereby publicly declare my
'Future woman and with whom
'I shall live with God's help
'Truly and happily until my end.'

"The bride said the same words. After this they sat down, and an aged man, who may have been the clerk of the meeting, stood up and said that this marriage was now legal and inseparable according to the laws of their church because no objection had been raised during the triple publication of their engagement and during the public promise of the engaged ones. Therefore he asked the assembled people to sign the marriage register as testimony. First, the parents of the couple signed, then others who so desired. I signed my name, as did some officers, and the ceremony was finished."[219]

Captain Ewald reported on a Quaker meeting in Philadelphia: "Since the Quakers were in the majority in Pennsylvania, I went today to a Quaker meeting next to my quarters, partly out of curiosity, partly to hear something good again. The meeting house was filled. Everybody was somber, and there was a hushed silence everywhere. I walked as softly as my boots, spurs, and big sword would permit, and stood for more than half an hour as quiet as a post. I was just about to leave, when suddenly an aged woman got up and asked the assembly to pay attention to her because the Holy Spirit had impelled her to say the following:

'My admonition is addressed to my sex. In these frightful times, which we have deserved by our sins, our land has been overrun by different foreign peoples. I hear very bad things of our wives and daughters. Wives and daughters are said to receive and pay visits to these soldiers. I know that some are not even ashamed to walk around with these people during the day. I pray you, mothers and fathers, stop these vices. Because these people are transients, you cannot take legal steps against them by our laws. If your daughters keep company with them, consider that you will have to accept to your own shame what they will leave behind for you. This is not good.'

"Then the matron sat down. Again there was silence for a while, whereupon the assembly left the place of devotion. I went to my quarters. My curiosity was satisfied, but I was not exactly edified." [220]

Major Baurmeister of the Hessian headquarters had a very high opinion of the Quakers in Philadelphia, and of General Washington, though not of Congress. He reported in May 1778: "On the 30th [of April] the rich and influential Quakers returned from their prisons, in which they had been confined from the time the rebels, after the action at Brandywine, were obliged to leave this city, and in which they were treated in no gentle manner. I cannot but tell your Lordship that the wives of four of these Quakers asked permission at the English headquarters to go and beg for the release of their husbands. General Washington, in camp at Valley Forge, received these courageous Quaker women in the most cordial manner, kept them for dinner, and for the rest of the day they were entertained by the General's wife. Through this lady's kindly intercession, all Quakers were released.

"The joy among the members of this powerful sect over the unexpected return to their brethren is extremely great. But how Congress treated them, and, according to good information, how many unworthy and previously worthless men make up this august body is shown by the fact that it completely forgot its dignity. Congress could not pass silently over this insult, yet, at the same time it could not praise enough the great justice of General Washington. And this praise is not unique; everyone is captivated by him." [221]

The activities of many American preachers for the cause of independence may account to some extent for the lack of favorable comment on religions other than that of the Quakers. Quartermaster Carl Bauer said that German preachers at Trenton, "wretchedly insulted the King of England" and "tried to convert everybody" to the cause of American independence.[222] Lieutenant Henkelmann, in a similar vein, wrote to his brother, who was a preacher: "It has been said that preachers have been abused. Not at all. They took their rifle and cartridge case with them to the pulpit and instructed their listeners clearly how to fight, and then left the church to go straight into battle." [223]

Lieutenant Colonel du Puy reported similar observations to Lieutenant General von Dittfurth in Marburg: "The clergymen are the dregs of the nation and they are the most active rebels. For example, one of them assured his flock a short time ago that it should have no fears about their future but should leave this up to him. He would take care of everything as long as the flock would bravely fight the Tories. He assured them that God is so interested in this war that the angels are dressed like riflemen." [224]

Lieutenant Henkelmann was astonished that some ministers in America did not wear robes as in Germany. He wrote to a friend in Cassel: "I could live here, but I like it better at home, because in Germany I never see a preacher who goes to church wearing his leather apron." [225]

Lieutenant Colonel von Dincklage wrote: "It is surprising that they hardly ever talk about religion, in spite of the variety of religions here. Most of them seem to be indifferent to religion, and many of them do not have more religion than their black slaves."[226]

Contact With Americans

When it was learned in America that Hessian and other German troops were going to fight on the side of the British, Congress, and other men of influence in America, tried to arouse the population against the mercenaries as well as against the British Crown for hiring them, and the German princes for letting them be hired.

Word about the alleged ferocity of the Hessian jaegers spread quickly.[227] As a result, the Hessians were viewed with panic. Because of the Hessian entry in the war, revolution-minded citizens became even more determined, and many of those who were still wavering became revolutionaries.[228] Upon their arrival, the Hessians saw, everywhere, the results of the American propaganda. Many of the inhabitants fled their homes at the rumored appearance of these so-called "barbarians" and "cannibals."

The Hessians had a taste of this when they were still on the high seas. Captain Ewald reported in his diary of an encounter with the captain and the surgeon of an American sea raider, which had been captured by an English frigate. He wrote: "The crew of the ship was dispersed among the fleet, and I got the captain and the doctor as my guests. They both trembled when they boarded the ship and looked upon me and other Hessians with the same attention and curiosity as you look upon monsters." [229]

Quartermaster Heusser gave an interesting account early in the war, of the result of the American propaganda. Heusser, who was captured the day after Christmas 1776 at Trenton, spent some days, together with other Hessian officers, in a ferry house on the Susquehanna River on the way to Virginia. From there he wrote: "Quickly the rumor spread that the captured Hessian officers were in the ferry house. This attracted a lot of troublesome visitors. There was hardly a person in the region who did not appear on horseback to see the men of whom he had heard so many dreadful things. But it could be seen in their faces that they regretted their journey. They had come to see monsters and realized that we looked like human beings. It is ridiculous, but it is true, that the people had such a terrible opinion of the Hessians that when they saw us they did not believe we were Hessians." [230]

Lieutenant Wiederholt told an amusing story based on the fear that was instilled in the Americans: "The so called [American] bull frog is as big as a partridge in Germany and has such a dreadful and awful voice that it resembles very much the bellow of a bull. An amusing story is told of that: At the beginning of the war some Light Dragoons of the enemy were sent on patrol to reconnoiter our encamped army, or rather, our advanced posts.... It happened that the silly Americans had an odd impression and fear of us Hessians. They did not believe that we looked like other human beings, but thought that we had a strange language and that we were a raw, wild, and barbaric nation.

"This patrol had to pass a forest at night, and they followed their route quietly and full of fear. They believed that they soon would approach our Hessian advance posts. Suddenly a bull frog croaked loudly. In dismay, they answered, 'Friend.' At this answer, the frog croaked a second time. They now believed that it was a Hessian picket, whereupon they stopped and cried 'Yes, yes, gentlemen, we are your prisoners'.... They got off their horses and waited for somebody to advance and take them prisoners.... Finally they realized their mistake and were ashamed and said: 'Goddamn, it is only a bull frog.' An officer of their army told me this story and we often laughed about it."[231]

Lieutenant Colonel von Dincklage reported while on Long Island in the summer of 1776 on American fears: "Most of the houses of this island were evacuated by their inhabitants. They had done so because of fear of the Hessians. They had such a terrible image of us that they even believed that we ate small children."[232]

All reports of Hessian observers showed that the American attitude soon changed. Quartermaster Kleinschmidt gave an interesting account of first steps toward mutual understanding: "You could see a secret fear in the inhabitants, which caused them to avoid contact with us; they even kept their wives and children in the houses and did not let them go out. In the course of time they became more friendly with us. They learned to understand our broken English, showed us their families, and laid aside their fear."[233]

A report of Captain Hinrichs described the beginnings of this change: "Tears of joy and gratitude ran down the faces of these formerly happy people when they found their houses, fruit, cattle, and all their furniture again and when I told them that I had only taken possession of it for them, and that I was going to hand it back to them."[234]

The disciplined behavior maintained among the Hessian troops was part of the reason for the change of mind of the American people. Before long it was noticed that Hessian officers found quarters in American homes more easily than their English comrades.[235]

Two passages from the diary of Captain von der Malsburg are indicative of the constantly improving relationship between the Hessians and the American people. As early as September 1776, he reported from Long Island: "We spend our lazy hours in the house of my companion.... We make good progress in the English language in his and his family's company. But he himself, and even more his wife, do not seem to be favoring the cause of the King. But if they really had a reason to come over to our side, I think, we should feel very much honored."[236]

Later the same year he wrote in New Jersey: "The inhabitants are well-mannered. As a rule they are naturally clearheaded, and some have even an enlightened intellect.... They have lost much of their initial reserve and shyness toward us after they found out that many of their ideas about us were wrong. But we can still clearly distinguish between the true partisans of the King; their behavior is open and friendly. Those who hide their hope for independence have secret ideas of liberty and do not receive us as friends. But they welcome all as well as they can, for hospitality is a conspicuous trait of the inhabitants of this continent."[237]

The efforts of many Hessian officers to become more proficient in the use of English so that contact with the American people would improve, bore fruit as the years passed.

The English commander in chief, General Howe, appointed the Hessian captain Baron Friedrich Ernst von Muenchhausen wing adjutant on his staff, and the Hessian Captain Maximilian Wilhelm O'Reilly was appointed town-major of New York by General Clinton for the winter of 1778-79.

COLONEL CARL EMIL ULRICH VON DONOP. *This tall, blond, young man does not appear to be the "monster" that the Americans expected to see when they rode many miles to look at the Hessian officers captured at Trenton. Although von Donop was in the Trenton-Bordentown area at the time of the capture, he was fortunate enough to escape. He is pictured here because he appears to be the only Hessian out of the 3000 men who were in the area of Trenton-Bordentown whose likeness has survived to show us what those captured Hessian officers might have looked like. Von Donop is shown here, shortly before he left for America with his troops. He is wearing his hunting garb and is holding his rifle. His dog is at his side, and von Donop is pointing to a rabbit that he had just bagged. The initials C.E.U. are engraved on the dog's collar. The painting is by Tischbein Jr.*

Captain Heinrich Wilhelm Reuting, another Hessian who held the post before O'Reilly, had resigned because of insufficient knowledge of the English language.238

It must have been an impressive indication of growing mutual esteem when the Hessian regimental band, captured at Trenton, was asked to play in Philadelphia at the 4th of July celebration in 1777.239

The war affected any one particular region of the country, mostly when fighting continued there for a long time. Once the fighting was over, life usually returned to normal rather fast. In occupied cities, the enemy was sometimes present for months or years; and, in some ways, created a business boom.

Major Baurmeister described this situation in Philadelphia in January 1778: "The city market is full of fresh meat, all kinds of fowl, and root vegetables. The residents of the city lack nothing except flour and firewood. What they sell and what they earn by working for so many people [the army of occupation] gives enough money to everyone to pay for even the most expensive things."240

Captain Ewald reported from Philadelphia about the same time: "A great part of the escaped inhabitants came gradually back to their homes. The city became lively, trade and commerce were blossoming again, and inhabitants and soldiers began to be reconciled to each other."241 Another report, that of Captain Hinrichs, also from Philadelphia, stated: "When we had held the city for just four weeks and the ships from New York arrived, everything became very lively, even livelier than during times of peace. Two out of three houses are shops."242

The merchants raised prices as the demand increased. Therefore, the Hessian officers harbored some resentment at this practice. Quartermaster Kleinschmidt wrote: "Prices are rising continuously, and we can do nothing about it and have to pay."243 Captain Hinrichs was similarly upset in Philadelphia over a trivial matter. He remarked that "...the haberdasher, is a special kind of creature.... He proclaims that the articles he sells are now in fashion and are selling well in England; therefore they should also sell well in Philadelphia, and other parts of America."244

A German officer remarked in a letter home that commercial life in New York increased considerably during the presence of English and German troops. He said: "I presume you will not believe that a carpenter earns 6 Rhenish Florins and more a day and a good coachman does not have to work for less than 400 Florins,245 including food and clothes.

"Maybe, you would like to be a chimney sweep. There is a royal chimney sweep here who tends to the chimneys of the army's quarters. He has half a dozen Negroes, each one of whom can sweep twenty chimneys a day and sometimes more. Mr. Chimney Sweep, who is sitting at home in comfort, is paid two York-Shillings for each chimney. The Negroes earn only enough for raw food and ragged clothes."246

Hinrichs wrote, also from New York: "There are only a few craftsmen now. The best ones are the hatters, shoemakers, and tailors, and of the artisans there are saddlers and goldsmiths. Nothing is known here of work in other materials such as ivory, steel, iron, stucco, bone, embroidery, and silk. Everything like this is from England, and is welcome."247

A friendly contact between Hessian soldiers and Americans was not always present. When on campaigns, the troops tended to infringe more upon the rights of the people than when in garrisons. Orders from Hessian commanders to maintain discipline and to leave the property of Americans untouched, were frequently issued.248 There were also orders decreeing that Americans be treated with consideration.249

Hessian journals mentioned some acts of lawlessness among the troops, but the accused, when found guilty, were always punished. Soldiers were even made to pay for stolen vegetables.250 When complaints about Hessian lawlessness (robbery or plundering), reached headquarters stricter controls were put into effect.251 Many of the minor offenses were committed by drunken soldiers, which called for special treatment, based on their past records.252

Only a few Hessian units were garrisoned at one place for a long period of time. In these occupied towns the inhabitants generally showed a Loyalistic attitude.253 This helped to establish a normal contact between the soldiers and the population. But when the soldiers, both British and Hessian, met hostile Americans in the field, there was frequent looting and extortion on both sides — the British and Hessians looting the Patriots and the Americans the Loyalists.254

As to lawlessness, it is necessary to distinguish between Hessian officers and rank and file soldiers. Since the officers were quartered in homes during the occupation of a town, they had closer contact with the population than did the common soldiers. They also acquired a better knowledge of the English language. And, since language difficulties were frequently the reason for misunderstandings and the resulting difficulties, officers ran into less trouble than did soldiers.

Some of the Hessians, mostly officers, married American girls.255 For example, Captain Friedrich von der Malsburg of the Regiment von Dittfurth, Captain Claudius Gerber of the Hesse-Hanau Free-Corps, Quartermaster Friedrich Jakob Kleinschmidt of the Regiment von Benning, Lieutenant Henkelmann of the Regiment von Seitz, and Lieutenant Wernicke of the Regiment von Porbeck married daughters of American Loyalists.256

An interesting incident regarding Hessian lack of resistance to rebel feminine American charm occurred in June 1780, during the invasion of New Jersey. The first division of British-Hessian troops to land at Elizabethtown from Staten Island was commanded by British Brigadier General Thomas Stirling. His division consisted of the British 37th and 38th Regiments, and the Hessian Leib and Landgraf Regiments.

General Stirling was wounded shortly after landing, and command of his division fell to Colonel Friedrich Wilhelm von Wurmb of the Leib Regiment. As Colonel Wurmb advanced up the road from Elizabethtown to Connecticut Farms at the head of his column, he approached the home of William Livingston, governor of New Jersey. When coming near the house, Colonel Wurmb saw a blooming rose bush climbing the porch trestle of the governor's house. These were bright red roses known as "blaze roses," which still bloom abundantly in New Jersey in mid-June.

Colonel Wurmb rode up to the house, accompanied by several officers and men, hoping to capture the governor. The governor's daughter, Susan, appeared at the door and told the colonel that only she and her sister were at home, whereupon Colonel Wurmb politely "asked leave to pick one" rose, which request Susan readily granted. The colonel then placed the rose in his hat and rode away.257

Hessian officers were given increased responsibility in America. Lieutenant General Wilhelm von Knyphausen was in charge of the troops in and around New York for almost a

LIBERTY HALL. *This painting by David M. Payne in 1970 shows the home of William Livingston, Revolutionary War governor of New Jersey, as it was during the war period, with two exceptions. The second floor of the wing at left was added as a bedroom for Mrs. Washington when she visited Liberty Hall enroute to her husband's first inaugural at New York in 1789. The second floor of the wing at right was added after 1856. It had been rumored for some time before the invasion of New Jersey in 1780, that a two thousand guinea reward had been offered for the capture of Livingston. In March 1779, Governor Livingston wrote to British General Clinton chiding him about the rumored offer. Because of this threat, the governor spent little time at Elizabethtown, which was frequently raided by armed parties from nearby Staten Island. The governor's family, however, remained much of their time at Liberty Hall during the war because they believed that it would be the best way to preserve their home. Courtesy Mrs. John Kean whose husband was a Livingston descendant through Susan Livingston, daughter of Peter van Brugh Livingston and niece of Governor Livingston.*

year and was highly respected because of his military conduct and his treatment of the people. When General von Knyphausen, in April 1782, gave up his New York post, and that of the Hessian High Command, because of illness, Colonel Friedrich Wilhelm von Wurmb wrote to the Hessian Minister of State, "We all love him...and the rebels talk of him with respect."[258]

A proclamation in 1779 issued by a group of citizens in Rhode Island showed their respect for the disciplined behavior of Hessian troops. It is in the form of a letter of gratitude to the Hessian commander in chief in Rhode Island, Major General Johann Christoph von Huyne:
"By the desire of the Inhabitants of Rhode Island.
To Major General de Huyn commanding the British and Hessian troops from Bavia Gate to Bristol Ferry:
"May it please Your Excellency to accept the most grateful thanks of the Inhabitants for the humanity, with which they have been treated, since Your Excellency took the Command, and be assured, Sir, they are sensible, that a father would not with more patience have heard the complaints of his children than Your Excellency has heard those of the Inhabitants, nor would have been more ready to have redressed them than Your Excellency, nor more effectually than Your Excellency has endeavoured to do by keeping the troops under Your command in the utmost discipline and good order imaginable.

"Be assured, Sir, in losing Your Excellency, we lose a gentleman, under whose protection and command we have been as happy, as those times would permit. And that Your Excellency may return to Your native-country loadened with riches and honor, and at last Your grey hair may descend to the grave in peace, beloved and respected by Prince and people, which is the sincere wishes of Your Excellency's most obedient servants, the subscribers,
[following are their names]
"Rhode Island, 1779, October 12."

Major General von Huyne thanked the signers of the above proclamation in a letter dated Rhode Island, 1779, October 15:
"To the inhabitants on Rhode Island
from the Bavia Gate to Bristol Ferry:
"Major General de Huyne accepts the sincere Thanks of the Inhabitants of this island for the Care, he is taken of them and their Property, since he has had the Command, and is happy to understand, that the Troops under his Command have behaved in such a Soldier-like manner, as to do Honor to their King, to the General and to the Officers that command them.

"The Inhabitants may depend on every Indulgence that can be granted by General Prescott, and they may also depend on General de Huyne to execute all Orders he may receive towards the Preservation of the Persons and property of the Inhabitants to the last Moment of our Stay on the Island.

"Given in my Quarter
at M. Taylors house the
15th Day of Octob. 1779.   De Huyne
                             Major General"[259]

Major General von Huyne did not take his honors back to Germany. He died in New York on July 26, 1780.[260]

The remarks of Captain Ewald, describing the departure of the last Hessian units from America seemed to speak for the majority of Hessians: "The flag with the thirteen stripes was flown everywhere, some salutes were fired, and all bells were ringing. The shores were loaded with people who threw their hats in the air, cried happily, and shouted with joy; they waved to us a happy journey with white scarfs. During all this there was deep silence on board the ships that were lying at anchor with troops, as if everyone were in deep mourning because of the loss of the thirteen beautiful provinces."[261]

Opinion of Americans

To evaluate the Hessian opinion of Americans we must keep in mind that as military opponents, it was difficult for the Hessians to have unbiased views. Further, being ideological adversaries of the American struggle for independence, they could not adequately assess its background. Even most of the Americans of that time may not have understood the full meaning of liberty and their struggle for independence.

As the contact between the Hessians and Americans became more friendly, the attitude of the Hessian common soldiers changed; but the ideas of most of the officers relative

REGIMENT VON HUYNE, LATER VON KNOBLAUCH. *This is the regiment that the residents of Bristol, R.I. thanked "for the humanity, with which they have been treated," during Hessian occupancy of their city. Apparently the men of this regiment got along well wherever they went. Shortly before the conclusion of the peace treaty, they were stationed in Savannah, Ga., and it was reported to Hessian headquarters that the men of this regiment "desert fast.... And the enemy have taken every care to encourage desertion as much as in their power...." Pictured here are the 1786 sketches of officer and enlisted man uniforms. [St AM E/195/2] Colors of the various elements are taken from a copy of the 1786 hand colored drawings in Hessian archives. They are: Coat: green; cuffs yellow; buttonholes lapeled and green; humeral ligament white. Waistcoat: green with red lining; sword belt white; buckle gold or yellow; officer's sash red. Pants: white. Shoes or boots: black. Hat: black with white drapery.*

to the struggle for independence remained quite firm. The persistent American propaganda, the defiant attitude of the American citizens who supported the cause of liberty, the guerilla tactics of American militiamen, and the defeats and large Hessian casualties embittered Hessian officers. These are perhaps the reasons why so few Hessian officers deserted. The Hessian manuscripts name only two ensigns as deserters; but actually there were a few more.[262] Some Hessian officers' resentment led to rather peculiar views. Captain Johann Hinrichs wrote from Philadelphia: "I have never seen so many foolish people as here. One reason for this may be that the food is not half as nourishing as it is at home. Milk has only half as much fat content, bread gives only insufficient strength."[263] Quartermaster Carl Bauer noted in South Carolina: "The male sex, especially in the countryside, is slim and rather tall, and, on the average, taller than the Europeans. There is nothing to be praised about the beauty of the female sex, for they are pale and I have only met a few with a fresh complexion.... Both sexes are indolent and not inclined to work."[264]

Major Baurmeister wrote: "The Americans are bold, unyielding and fearless. They have always lived in plenty, and we cannot block their resources. Then their indomitable ideas of liberty, the main springs of which are held and guided by every hand in Congress! Good for nothing and unimportant as most of these men may have been before these disturbances (because they were incompetent and without wealth) they now resort to every means for more than one reason, to weaken the rich and the Loyalists within and stubbornly resist the English without."[265] Colonel Ludwig von Wurmb wrote to von Jungkenn in January 1778: "There are bad people in this country, and the women must be blamed for inflaming the young men by bestowing upon them the pretty name of 'sons of liberty.' When I was in Europe, I had pity on them, but now no more. They have been the happiest people under the sun.

"They did not have to give any of their property to the King. Only landowners paid a little excise tax. This war has been caused by arrogance, pride, and foolishness on the side of the Americans and by negligence on the side of the English. No matter how it ends, they will never be as happy as they have been. The Americans are like father Adam who had to leave paradise because of wantonness."[266]

An unknown Hessian officer wrote the following about the Americans: "Everybody at home who takes their side and believes that they had good reasons for this rebellion should live with them for a while to be punished for this attitude and should also read their constitution. It permits the worst man to live here like the richest man at home, with little work. He would probably soon speak in a different tone and agree with me that not need but wickedness and wantonness are the cause of the whole rebellion.

"In spite of the fact that most of them descend from ragamuffins and scamps who were expelled from some other country, they are so haughty here and live everywhere, especially in New York, in grand style.... Their wealth is increasing daily, because they get so much money from the troops, and they do not even give a soldier a grain of salt without charging for it. In this situation nothing is more annoying than the fact that these people, who are rebels, have been treated politely by the soldiers on strict orders of the King."[267]

Many Hessian officers combined their judgment of the Revolution and of the Americans with critical remarks on the state of war and the American chances to win it. Some high-ranking officers thought, up to the very last moment, that the British were going to suppress the rebellion by a military victory. Others lost more and more confidence in a British success as the war went on.

The third Hessian commander in chief, Lieutenant General Friedrich Wilhelm von Lossberg, at that time a major general, wrote in November 1777 from Rhode Island: "Personally I do not see when the rebellion will come to an end. We have to deal with a whole continent and as long as there is one person left, he will be a rebel with all his heart, even if he is not allowed to show it. There are clever men among them and they only need money. But they do have enough artillery ammunition and food, and they are learning more and more how to fight... but what does it help them?... We fight for the right cause, and Heaven does not forsake Germans. In a war not everything can go as well as one could wish; otherwise we would have put an end to it very quickly."268

Only two months later von Lossberg wrote: "It seems that we are far from an anticipated peace because the bitterness of the rebels is too widespread, and in regions where we are masters the rebellious spirit is still in them. The land is too large, and there are too many people. The more land we win, the weaker our army gets in the field. It would be best to come to any agreement with them."269

Major Baurmeister was also impressed by the growing resolution of the Americans. He reported from Philadelphia in January 1778 on the encampment of the Continental Army at Valley Forge: "With the greater part of his army he [General Washington] occupies a stationary camp at Valley Forge, where the soldiers have been encouraged with cash rewards to build solid huts. They have been told, moreover, that their steadfastness and patience through one more campaign will secure their independence once and for all. They also enjoy the generous support of foreign powers [the French], who have their staple in Boston. Furthermore, they have more means of their own to keep up this war than was at first supposed."270

Colonel Ludwig von Wurmb saw another reason for the American steadfastness and resoluteness. He doubted that they would want to come to an agreement with the British: "When people who were shoemakers, tailors, and innkeepers become generals and members of Congress, they do not like to take up their old professions again...."271

The opinions of the diarists were also colored by a growing war-weariness. Lieutenant General von Knyphausen wrote in April 1778 from Philadelphia to von Jungkenn: "...in spite of the fact that farmers, craftsmen, and tradesmen in general seem to want peace and accept the proposed conditions, it is believed here that Congress will not consent but insist on independence. A war between England and France, of which rumor is spreading would probably stiffen their obstinacy."272

Colonel von Wurmb wrote in January 1779 from Flushing, Long Island: "I wish we were out of this miserable country with honor.... There is an infamous sort of people in Congress. If a man does not follow their dictates, he is summoned before a court and hanged. In Philadelphia they hanged a son, Robert, of a good friend of mine because he had said that Congress was not being fair to England, for this country owed everything to England."273 Major Baurmeister reported to Cassel from New York in July 1781: "Everyone wishes, as much as a soldier has a right to wish, that he may soon return home."274

The determination of the Americans impressed the Hessians despite reservations concerning the Revolution. They simply could not understand why Americans should risk their lives in the struggle for independence. Captain Hinrichs wrote to Professor Schloezer: "You know about the Huguenot Wars in France. What they called 'religion', is here 'liberty', the same fanaticism, the same furious events."275

Quartermaster Kleinschmidt reported that the Americans celebrated the first Independence Day on July 4, 1777, with a cannonade throughout the country except New York, which was occupied by the British: "One inhabitant there, who could not hide the fact that he was a 'rebel', showed his happiness, and was punished. General Prescott sentenced him to four weeks imprisonment."276 Major Baurmeister wrote of the inhabitants of South Carolina: "I wish I had the space ... to describe the obstinacy with which nearly all show themselves to be rebels."277

Von der Malsburg got much closer to the roots of the American struggle for independence: "Earlier [than Europeans] they reach the maturity of body and soul. They have special intellectual powers and a better kind of knowledge in various fields. It is a rare man who does not own a collection of all sorts of instructive books and has read them to advantage. I have even been assured that no Member of Parliament in London knows more about the momentary political situation of this country than, probably without exception, each inhabitant here. The form of government depends only on thinkers."278

Other comments of Hessian officers showed a mixture of contempt and respect. One officer wrote: "In the beginning I tended to be well-disposed towards the Americans. Prejudices and false concepts of the suppression under which they lived — as German papers always defended their cause — brought me over to their side. But since I had a chance to learn something of their history, their motives for this war, and their character, I have no longer a good opinion of them.

"Their most abominable trait of character is ingratitude. It is true when they tell you, how happily, peacefully and carefree they had lived at the bosom of charitable nature before the outbreak of these miserable disturbances. One is almost inclined to consider the Britons to be tyrants, who could not stand to see their descendants being happy. This is the way they explain it to you. But once you become informed of the unburdened care with which the motherland guarded her colonies since their beginning, the story is a very different one.

"She had to wage ugly and costly wars for the cause of peace and security, now with the Indians, now with neighboring European nations, while the Americans were calmly looking on. Consider also the great sums she spent for their civil institutions, salaries, churches, schools, academies, etc. When she rightfully asked that the Americans bear some of the load, which was properly theirs, the children rebelled against their mother.

"The resistance against illegal taxes was nothing more than a masquerade at the beginning. The plan of the rebellion is older and more deeply rooted. It was born primarily in the provinces of New England. Since these people are mostly Presbyterians and Puritans, every government on earth, especially that of a king, was a thorn in their sides because of their religious principles."279

The following remarks by Lieutenant Colonel von Dincklage, though more detailed, are typical of those of his fellow officers. Von Dincklage wrote: "Peace has probably left this once happy country forever. They may have peace but not happiness when the war is over. It matters little whether the Americans win or lose. Presently this country is the scene of the most cruel events. Neighbors are on opposite sides, children are against their fathers. Anyone who differs with the opinions of Congress in thought or in speech is regarded as an enemy and turned over to the hangman, or else he must flee.

"We give these refugees food, and support most of them with arms. They go on patrol for us in small groups and then escape into their home districts to take revenge by pillaging, murdering, and burning. The refugee Loyalists who escape to the savages make common cause with them and carry out the most cruel devastations.

"If peace comes after an English victory, discord between the two parties will flare up underneath the ashes and nobody will be able to resolve it. If the rebels should win, they will break their necks, one by one. What misery the people have plunged themselves into!

"The inhabitants lived in true liberty before the rebellion and had to pay only a few taxes or none at all. The government imposed upon them only taxes for imported luxury articles, but articles which they could still buy cheaper than the English in England. The landowners gave in taxes what they wanted to give. This money was spent for public welfare, such as roads and buildings, and for support of the administration. In one word, no nation could live more happily. But in what kind of situation are they now? It may end either way, and even worse for them if they get their so-called freedom. Nowadays, you cannot even think without being penalized. If somebody says something different from what Congress commands, he may go to the gallows.

"Now the Americans have to pay immense sums to maintain land and sea power and have to burden themselves with great debts. Some private persons profit by the change, such as merchants, bankrupted business men, and lawyers. These are the men who have incited the revolution. Heaven, which grants nothing without wise design, knows that man here on earth cannot endure perfect happiness and that it does not agree with him because of his corruptible nature."[280]

Some Hessian officers believed that the revolutionary ideas were the product of a small group of interested men, and consequently thought that the war could end without a British military victory. Colonel Johann Friedrich von Cochenhausen of the Erb Prinz Regiment wrote in the summer of 1778 from Philadelphia: "Many and probably most of the Americans are not happy about the news of the treaty with France, which was made public here. In the hearts of most of them there is still the fire of an old love for the motherland.... It is even said that in Connecticut, the state where the revolution originated, many people talk of a peaceful settlement."[281]

Many Hessian officers began to realize that Britain could not win the war after France had become a party to it. They reacted with bitter comments. A song, which originated among the Hessian troops in Rhode Island, ridiculed the French and the Americans and scoffed at the new treaty as ineffective.[282]

After the peace treaty was signed and the British and Hessian troops were ready to leave America, Major Baurmeister commented as follows on the relations between Americans and the French: "The extent of commerce with Great Britain along the American coast has not yet been determined, and it would seem that other nations would profit in trade from the nonexistence of such an agreement. That this is not the case is due particularly to the Americans' decided preference for British merchandise.

"The merchants of other countries, especially those of France, assure everyone in the maritime towns that taste for British wares is a pernicious prejudice, but to no avail. The Americans are not deceived by such make-believe. To be sure, they appreciate the spirit they have acquired from the French and are malicious enough to give crude expression to the cunning they have learned; but these crude people lack the manners to be able to conceal the deep-seated hatred they feel toward the French. Dr. Franklin has warned Congress to guard carefully against any French encroachments. Washington always kept a certain distance from the auxiliaries and whenever General Rochambeau made a proposal, asked time to think it over."[283]

Disillusioned with the state of the war, far from home, and exhausted by the hardships of the campaigns, many Hessian officers longed for the end of the war, especially after the American-French decisive victory at Yorktown. Their attitude toward the Americans became more objective and their remarks somewhat less prejudiced.

HESSIAN ARTIFACTS. *Pictured here are two embossed brass cartridge box ornaments from the Erb Prinz (top) and von Bose (bottom) regiments, which were excavated at Yorktown, Va. Related to this find, Major Baurmeister wrote on November 6, 1781, about two weeks after the Battle of Yorktown, as follows: "It is not known how many killed and wounded Lord Cornwallis had between the 27th of September and the day of capitulation. The Erb Prinz Regiment had Surgeon [Franz August] Bauer and twenty-three men killed, sixty-two wounded, and three deserters, while von Bose's Regiment had Captain [Herman Christian] Roll and sixteen men killed and Ensign Spangenberg and forty men wounded." Courtesy Colonial National Historical Park, National Park Service.*

Colonel Ludwig von Wurmb wrote to von Jungkenn five months after Yorktown: "...I think that England would do best to come to terms with America one way or another.... When the troops are ready to return to Hesse and there should be no other war, I would like all foreigners [i.e. non-Hessians] to get permission to stay here if they so desire. Otherwise they will desert and take their rifles with them. I would suggest that all mounted foreigners and all craftsmen remain behind because they would have good opportunities here in times of peace...."[284]

In his last letter from America, October 5, 1783, just before departing with the last Hessian troops to go home, Major Baurmeister summed up his final impressions of the country where Hessian soldiers had stayed for more than seven years:

"General Washington lives near Princeton, like a private individual. If, as is generally said, he gave prestige to the American army, it is certain that his frequent presence near Princeton is lending some dignity and respect to the declining Congress [then located at Princeton]. As a matter of fact this great council has never been so little respected and revered as it now is, especially in New England, where the prescribed taxes cannot be collected. This is now also the case in Pennsylvania, where Congress's flight from Philadelphia is considered an unpardonable mistake. Besides, the Pennsylvanians were the first to realize that the members of Congress were misappropriating the money gained from the sale of confiscated property.

"In view of the present misgovernment, General Washington could obtain anything he might want, even the crown of North America. The people are ready to offer it to him, but so far he has shown no desire for this gift of fortune, if, indeed, it is one."[285]

ROCKINGHAM, WASHINGTON'S HEADQUARTERS. *It was this house, called Rockingham, at Rocky Hill, New Jersey, a short distance from Princeton, to which Major Baurmeister referred when he wrote, "General Washington lives near Princeton like a private individual." Washington arrived at Rockingham on August 23, 1783, at the request of the Continental Congress, which was in session at Princeton. The reason for Congress's presence there was that on June 21, unpaid soldiers in Philadelphia had rioted in that capital city, and they continued to riot until the 24th, when the Congress resolved to adjourn to a safer place. Washington remained at Rockingham until November 10, when he departed for West Point, there to await the evacuation of New York City by the British and German auxiliary forces, which occurred on November 25, 1783. Courtesy Division of Parks, Forestry & Recreation, State of New Jersey.*

BIBLIOGRAPHY

HESSIAN MANUSCRIPTS

StAM Hessisches Staatsarchiv Marburg, Germany.
Bestand 4h, Verzeichnis 409
no. 3: Journal vom Hessischen Corps in Amerika unter dem General von Heister, 1776 - 1777.
Verzeichnis 410
no. 1: Relationes vom Nordamerikanischen Kriege unter dem Commando des General von Heister, 1776, 1777, vol. I.
no. 2: Relationes vom Nord-Amerikanischen Kriege unter dem Commandeur General von Knyphausen, 1777, 1778, vol. II.
Verzeichnis 411
no. 1: Relationes vom Nord-Amerikanischen Kriege unter dem Commandir. General von Knyphausen, 1779, 1780, vol. III.
no. 2: Relationes vom Nord-Amerikanischen Kriege unter dem Commandir. General von Knyphausen, 1781, 1782, vol. IV.
no. 3: Relationes vom Nord-Amerikanischen Kriege unter dem Commandir. General von Lossberg, 1783, 1784, vol. V.
Verzeichnis 412
no. 2: Journal vom Hochloeblichen Regiment Prinz Carl, 1776-1784.
no. 3: Journal von der Campagne in Amerika, Tom. I, 1776-1783.
no. 4: Journal von der Campagne in Amerika, Tom. II.
no. 5: Journal von der Campagne in Amerika, Tom. III.
Verzeichnis 413
no. 2: Journals und Relationes von der Campagne in Amerika, Tom. IV.
no. 4: Journal von der Campagne in Amerika, Tom. VI.
Verzeichnis 415
no. 5: Militaerberichte und Relationen von den Operationen der hessischen Korps im amerikanischen Kriege, 1776-1782.
Bestand 12, Verzeichnis 11
No. 1 Feldzug in Amerika, 1776-1784.
no. 1a: Oberkommando.
no. 1b: Darstellung der Affaire in Trenton durch den Gen.-Lt. von Heister.
no. 1c: dto, von den einzelnen Truppenteilen.
no. 2: Journal des Hochloeblichen Regimentes von Alt-Lossberg.
no. 4: Journal des (von Wutgenau'schen) Leib-Inf. Rgts. von Kospoth.
no. 5: Journal von dem Hochloeblichen Regiment von Donop, modo von Knyphausen.
no. 6: Journal des Inf.-Regiments von Knyphausen.
no. 7: Journal von dem Hochfuerstlich-Hessischen Hochloeblichen Infanterie Regiment von Truembach, modo General-Lieutenant von Bose.
no. 9: Ordre Buch vom Hochloeblichen Regiment von Mirbach.
no. 10: Journal ueber die merkwuerdigen Vorfa-

elle bey dem Hochloeblichen Leib Infanterie Regiment modo Erbprinz.

no. 12: Journal von dem Hochfuerstlich Hessischen des General Major von Knoblauch Loebl. Garnisons [Regiment].

no. 13: Journal vom Loeblichen Garnisons-Regiment von Huyn, nachher von Benning.

no. 15: Journal von dem Hochloebl.-Hessischen Grenadier Battaillon olim von Minnigerode, modo von Loebenstein.

no. 16: Journal, Vom Hochfuerstlich-Hessischen Grenadier-Battaillon Platte.

no. 17: Journal, gefuehrt bey dem Hochloeblich Hessischen Feld-Jaeger Corps.

no. 18: Ordres (Fuer das hessen-hanauische Feldjaeger-Korps).

JP   Von Jungkenn Papers, 7 vols., William L. Clements Library, Ann Arbor, Michigan.

Ewald   Ewald, Johann (von), *Tagebuch von dem amerikanischen Kriege* 4 vols. Library of His Highness Friedrich Ferdinand, Prince of Schleswig-Holstein, Glucksburg/Ostsee, Germany.

AMERICAN MANUSCRIPTS

WCL   William L. Clements Library, Ann Arbor, Michigan, Shelburne Papers.

LC   Library of Congress, Washington, D.C.

NYPL   New York Public Library, New York, N.Y.

PRINTED SOURCES

1. Baurmeister, Carl Leopold (von), *Confidential Letters and Journals 1776 - 1784 of Adjutant General Major Baurmeister of the Hessian Forces*, in: Uhlendorf, Bernhard A., *Revolution in America*, New Brunswick, N.J. 1957.

2. *Deutsch-Amerikanische Geschichtsblaetter, German-American Historical Review*, Jahrbuch der Deutsch-Amerikanischen Historischen Gesellschaft von Illinois, vol. XX-XXI, Chicago, Ill., 1922:

     p. 251 : "Two letters from Halifax 1783," A. Woringer ed.

     p. 253 : "Journal des Corps von Heister"

     p. 253-256: "Journal des Obersten Baurmeister"

     p. 256 : "Aktenstuecke und Aufzeichnungen der Brigade Mirbach."

     p. 257 : "Journal des Gren. Btl. Platte."

     p. 258-261: "Tagebuch des Regiments von Lossberg."

     p. 261-263: "Journal des Leib-Regiments, nachher Erbprinz."

     p. 263-266: "Tagebuch des Oberstleutnants von Dinklage."

     p. 267-278: "Tagebuch des Gren. Btl. Platte."

     p. 278-280: "Tagebuch des Regt. von Huyne."

     p. 280-304: "Protokoll der Amtshandlungen des Feldpredigers G.C. Coester bei den Regt. von Donop und von Lossberg."

vol. XXVII-XXVIII, Chicago, Ill., 1928: "Tagebuch eines hessischen Offiziers, Heinrich von Bardeleben."

3. Heister, Lt. von, ed., "Aus dem Tagebuch eines vormaligen kurhessischen Offiziers ueber den Nordamerikanischen Freiheitskrieg 1776 - 1777," in: *Zeitschrift fuer Kunst, Wissenschaft und Geschichte des Krieges*, vol. 3, Berlin, 1828, p. 223-270.

4. Henkelmann, Johannes Heinrich, Lt., "Brief an Lt. Georg Bauer aus Halifax," A. Woringer ed., in: *Hessenland*, 24, 1906, p. 339-341.

5. Hinrichs, Johannes, Stabs-Kapitaen, "Auszug aus dem Hand Journal (Extract from the Private Journal of Staff Captain Hinrichs of the Jaeger Corps)," in: Bernhard A. Uhlendorf, *Siege of Charleston*, Ann Arbor, Michigan, 1938, p. 107-363.

6. Koester, G.C., "Aus dem Tagebuch des Feldpredigers in Regiment von Donop und von Lossberg," in: *Mitteilungen an die Mitglieder des Vereins fuer hessische Geschichte*, vol. 24, 1901.

7. Kuemmel, Heinrich, Feldprediger, "Aus dem Tagebuch," Otto Gerlandt ed., in: *Hessenland*, vol. 6, 1894, p. 72-76; vol. 7, 1894, p. 87-91.

8. Riedesel, Frederike Charlotte Louise, Freifrau von, *Die Berufsreise nach Amerika*, Berlin 1801. English edition: Marvin L. Brown Jr. ed., *Baroness von Riedsel and the American Revolution*, University of North Carolina Press, Chapel Hill, 1965.

9. Schloezer, August Ludwig, *Briefwechsel meist historischen und politischen Inhalts*, vol. I-X, 1776-1781, no. 1-60, Goettingen 1780-1782.

10. Schloezer, August Ludwig, *Stats-Anzeigen*, vol. I-X, no. 1-60, Goettingen 1782-1787.

11. Schoepf, Johann David, *Reise durch einige der mittleren und suedlichen vereinigten nordamerikanischen Staaten nach Ost-Florida und den Bahama-Inseln, unternommen in den Jahren 1783 und 1784*, part I/II, Erlangen, 1788.

12. Schubarth, Martin Christian Friedrich Daniel, *Deutsche Chronik auf das Jahr 1774-1777*, Augsburg and Ulm 1774-1777.

13. Wiederholt, Andreas, "Tagebuch" (Diary of Captain Wiederholt of the von Knyphausen Regiment), M.D. Learned and C. Grosse eds., in *Americana Germanica*, vol. IV, 1, New York, London and Berlin 1902, p. 1-93.

NEWSPAPERS

1. *Muenchner Zeitung*, Munich, 1775-1777.
2. *Augspurgische Ordinari Postzeitung*, Augsburg, 1774-76
3. *New Jersey Journal*, Chatham, N.J. Feb. 16, 1779.

LITERATURE

1. Anderson, Troyer Steele, *The Command of the Howe Brothers during the American Revolution*, New York, London and Oxford, 1936.

2. Bowman, Allan, "The Morale of the American Revolutionary Army," in: *American Council on Public Affairs*, Washington, D.C., 1943.

3. Davidson, Philipp, *Propaganda and the American Revolution, 1763 - 1783*, Chapel Hill, 1941.

4. Ditfurth, Franz Wilhelm, Freiherr von, *Historische Volkslieder der Zeit von 1756-1871*, vol. I, part 2, Berlin, 1872.

5. Faust, Albert Bernhardt, *Das Deutschtum in den Vereinigten Staaten in seiner geschichtlichen Bedeutung*, Leipzig, 1912. Original English edition: *The German Element in the United States*, 2 vols., Boston & New York, 1909.

6. Kipping, Ernst, *Die Truppen von Hessen-Kassel im amerikanischen Unabhaengigkeitskrieg 1776-1783*, Darmstadt, 1965.

7. Lith, Freiherr von der, "Feldzug der Hessen nach Amerika," in: *Ephemeriden ueber Aufklaerung, Literatur und Kunst*, vol. II, Marburg, 1785, p. 1-60.

8. Loeher, Franz, *Geschichte und Zustaende der Deutschen in Amerika*, Cincinnati, 1847, Goettingen, 1855.

9. Moore, Frank, *Diary of the American Revolution, from Newspapers and Original Documents*, 2 vols., New York & London, 1860.

10. Smith, Samuel S. *The Battle of Trenton*, Monmouth Beach, N.J., 1965.

ANNOTATIONS

JP   von Jungkenn Papers, W.L. Clements Library, Ann Arbor, Mich.
LC   Library of Congress, Washington, D.C.
NYPL   New York Public Library, New York, N.Y.
St AM   Hessian State Archives, Marburg, Germany
WCL   William L. Clements Library, Ann Arbor, Mich.

1) StAM 10.2.36
2) Article no. 3 of the treaty
3) StAM 12, 1 Ba 15, Journal of Grenadier Battalion von Minnigerode p. 2; Cf. Battle order
4) StAM 4h.409.3., p. 3f; Cf. Battle order
5) Ibid., 4h.411.3., p. 144; Cf. Battle order
6) Ibid., 10.2.36
7) Ibid., 4h. 331.4
8) Ibid., 13.A.6., no. 200, article no. 4
9) Ibid., 4h.410.2, Knyphausen and Landgrave Friedrich II, New York, 1778, Aug. 13
10) Ibid., 12.11. I Ba 15
11) Ibid., 12.2. 8529, Cassel, 1776, Nov. 19
12) Ibid., 4h.328/I, Cassel, 1782, Apr. 13, p. 102
13) Loc. cit.
14) StAM 4h.328/I, Ziegenhain, 1782, Apr. 28, p. 106
15) JP 6:12, L.J.A. v. Wurmb, 1778, Aug. 23-31
16) JP 6:18/19, H.C. Fenner, Halifax, 1782, Oct. 24
17) Ewald, Diary, vol. I, p. 282f., 1777, Nov. 27
18) Ibid., vol. II, p. 42, 1778, May 16
19) StAM 4h.328. 158/I, p. 52, Lt Gen v. Gohr to the Landgrave Ziegenhain, 1782, Sept. 6
20) Landgrave Friedrich II
21) Seume, Johann Gottfried, *Mein Leben*, Bremen, Schuenemann 1964, p. 51-52
22) JP 3:2, L.J.A. v. Wurmb, 1779, Oct. 26
23) JP 4:56. Halifax, 1781, Sept. 21
24) JP 3:30, Bremerlehe on board *Charming Nancy*, 1780, June 2
25) JP 7:1, 1776, May 17
26) StAM 13.215., p.3, order no. 9
27) JP 7:16, Friedrich Carl Ludwig von Linder, Journal, 1782, June 11-Aug. 15
28) JP 3:60, von Knyphausen, New York, 1780, Oct. 28; JP 4:51, Baurmeister, New York, 1781, Aug. 19; JP 7:16, von Linder, Journal, 1782, June-Aug.
29) StAM 4h.328.151., p. 3, no. 154
30) Ibid., 12.2.8527
31) JP 1:72, Philadelphia, 1778, May 10
32) WCL, Miscellaneous Collection, Hessian Soldier, 77/78
33) JP 2:42, 1779, Jan. 18
34) JP 2:46, 1779, Feb. 5
35) JP 2:50, 1779, Feb. 25
36) StAM 4h.410.1, Headquarters, Staten Island, 1776, Aug. 16
37) In the winter of 1777-78, the troops were in winter quarters from Nov. 18 till May 25, Ewald, Diary, vol. I, p. 114, 129
38) StAM 4h.409.3, order no. 4
39) Ibid., 4h.411.3
40) Ibid., 12.11. I Ba 9, p. 12
41) Ibid., 12.11. I Ba 12, 1778, Sept. 7
42) JP 4:52, 1781, Aug. 27, Max von Westerhagen to Landgrave Friedrich; ibid., 6:24, 1782, Oct. 31, Friedrich von Porbeck to von Jungkenn
43) StAM 12.11. I Ba, la, Philadelphia, 1777, Dec. 15
44) Ibid., 9, p. 10
45) Ibid., 12, 1777, Oct. 31
46) Ibid., 18, p. 43
47) JP 7:5, Baurmeister, Philadelphia, 1777, July 20-Oct. 17
48) StAM 4h.410.2, Hills House near Germantown, 1777, Oct. 13
49) Ibid., 4h.411.3, New York, 1782, Aug.6
50) JP 7:5, Baurmeister, Philadelphia, 1777, July 20-Oct. 17
51) StAM 12.11, I Ba 17, p. 90
52) Ewald, Diary, vol. I, p. 162, 287
53) *Report on American Manuscripts in the Royal Institution of Great Britain* vol. II, (Dublin 1906), p. 210-211. On board the *Romulus*, Hampton Road, 1780, Nov. 19
54) StAM 4h.411.3, p. 206f., New York, 1783, Nov. 1
55) Ibid., 13.A.6, no. 232, p. 2
56) Loc. cit.
57) JP 2:30. In camp on Spuyten Duyvil, 1778, Nov. 6
58) JP 3:7, York Island [Manhattan], 1779, Nov. 28
59) JP 3:28, Hans von Knoblauch. On the Weser River near Nienburg, 1780, May 24
60) StAM 12.11.la
61) JP 5:41, Savannah, Friedrich von Porbeck, 1782, March [?]
     JP 5:43, Hans von Knoblauch, Charleston, 1782, Apr. 20
62) JP 6:31, Friedrich Ludwig von Benning, Charleston, 1782, Nov. 27
63) JP 6:45, New York, 1783, Apr. 13
64) JP 6:46, New York, 1783, Apr. 29
65) JP 2:29, Friedrich Wilhelm von Lossberg, Newport, R.I., 1778, Nov. 6
66) JP 5:23, Friedrich von Porbeck, Savannah, 1782, Feb. 22
67) JP 3:79, Ludwig Johann Adolph von Wurmb, Westbury, Long Island, 1781, Feb. 17
68) What appears to be the only extant copy of such a handbill, (in the German language), distributed to the Hessians on Staten Island in August 1776, is in the State Archives at Marburg.
69) Savannah, Ga.; Colonel Alured Clarke
70) *Report on American Manuscripts in the Royal Institution of Great Britain*, vol. II, (Dublin 1906) p. 418, Camp Davis's House, 1782, Mar. 12
71) JP 2:51, New York, 1779, Feb. 27
72) JP 5:25; Proclamation of John Martin, Governor of Georgia, of which a translation is enclosed in Porbeck's letter of 1782, March 2
73) LC, US-Revolution, III, 20-M-1
74) The Address of Cpt. Bowen to the Brunswick and Hesse Hanau Prisoners of War, Reading, 1782, July 30; WCL, Shelburne Papers, vol. 69, 9. 120-124
75) Extract of Instructions from the Honble the Minister of Finance of the United States of America, and the Honble the Secretary of the Board of War, dated at Philadelphia the 11th day of July 1782; WCL, Shelburne Papers, vol. 69, p. 117-119
76) LC, US-Revolution, II, 20-M-1
77) JP 6:4, Baurmeister, New York, 1782, Aug. 10
78) Hessian Major Friedrich Heinrich Scheer
79) Hessian Lt Col Johann Christian du Puy or du Buy
80) JP 6:48, New York, 1783, June 1
81) JP 6:50, New York, 1783, July 25
82) *Augspurgiscne Ordinari Postzeitung*, Augsburg, 1774, Aug. 24, 27
83) 1776, June 18, cited in Uhlendorf, *Revolution in America*, p. 11
84) Dittfurth, Franz Wilhelm, *Historische Volkslieder der Zeit von 1756-1871*, vol. II, pt 2, Berlin 1872, p. 370-373
85) Killy, Walter, *Ein Deutsches Lesebuch* I, 1750-1786, Frankfurt/M, 1962, p. 63
86) Dittfurth, op. cit. p. 5-7
87) Ibid., p. 7-8
88) Ibid., p. 9
89) Ibid., p. 4-5
90) *Muenchner Zeitung*, Munich, 1776, Nov. 15
91) Probably the Austrian War of Succession or the Seven Years War
92) *Augspurgische Postzeitung*, 1774, Dec. 1
93) Ibid., 1776, June 28
94) Aus dem Tagebuch eines vormaligen kurhessischen Officiers ueber den nordamerikanischen Unabhaengigkeitskrieg, 1776-1777, Lt. von Heister ed., p. 223f
95) Bardeleben, *Deutsch-Amerikanische Geschichtsblaetter*, vol. XXVII-XXVIII, p. 56
96) StAM 12.11. I Ba 2, 1776, Aug. 25
97) StAM 4h, 412.3
98) Schloezer, I/2, O. 103f
99) StAM 12.11. I Ba 16, p. 150, 1776, Oct. 21
100) The first lightning rod in Europe was mounted on Eddystone Lighthouse near Plymouth, England. The first used in Germany, in 1769, was on the spire of St. Jacob Church in Hamburg
101) Schloezer, I/2., p. 108
102) StAM 4h,410.1, p. 398-401, Von Heister to the Landgrave, New York, 1776, Dec. 22
103) Ibid., 12.11. I Ba 16, p. 100f; 1776, Oct. 28
104) Ibid., p. 122; 1776, Dec. 28
105) Ibid., p. 146f; 1777, June 30
106) NYPL, Hess. Ms., no. 26, and LC, box no. 2385; Ms. Hass. 40 no. 284/85 (Copy) In the following only the diary at the NYPL is cited
107) Uhlendorf, *Siege of Charleston*, p. 144-159; p. 318-363
108) *Briefwechsel* and *Statsanzeiger*
109) Uhlendorf, *Revolution in America*, a complete edition of Baurmeister's letters in English translation. Of the diaries of von Muenchhausen and von der Malsburg, there are copies in the NYPL. The first is in preparation for publication by Philip Freneau Press.
110) JP 1:24, 1777, Jan. 5
111) Schloezer, I/3, p. 32, Rhode Island, 1777, June 24
112) Kuemmel, Heinrich, From the Diary of the Field-Chaplain, p. 75
113) NYPL, Hess. Ms., no. 26
114) Ibid., no. 33a, p. 366-368
115) StAM 4h.410.1. - Von Heister to the Landgrave, New York, 1776, Dec. 22
116) Ibid., 4h.413.4, extract of a letter of Lt. Henkelmann to secretary Strieder in Cassel; In the camp at Fort Knyphausen 1777, Jan. 1
117) Ibid., 12.11. I Ba 16, p. 91-93
118) A heller, a german copper coin at the end of the 18th century, was the smallest piece of currency
119) StAM 12.11. I Ba 16, p. 35
120) Ibid., p. 27f
121) NYPL Hess. Ms., no. 26
122) Schloezer, I/4, p. 116, On the Neck near Philadelphia, 1778, June 2
123) StAM 12.11. I Ba 6, 1777, Oct. 24
124) Ibid., la, In the camp near Philadelphia, 1777, Nov. 3
125) NYPL, Hess. Ms., no. 26
126) JP 1:42, 1777, Aug. 31
127) NYPL, Hess. Ms. no. 4, no. 30a, 30b.: Geschichte des Hochloeblichen Fuesilier Regiments von Lossberg in Form eines Tagebuchs, p. 30-33
128) Ewald, Diary, vol. IV, p. 182
129) Ibid., vol. III, p. 195
130) StAM I Ba 16, p. 296f; I Ba 13, p. 125
131) Loc. cit.
132) NYPL, Hess. Ms. no. 26
133) StAM 12.11. I Ba 13, p. 125
134) NYPL, Hess. Ms. no. 27, p.63
135) Schloezer, I/5, p. 6, S.H.D., Auditor to Professor Schloezer, Savannah, 1779, Jan. 16
136) StAM 12.11. I Ba 15, p. 119
137) NYPL, Hess. Ms. no. 33a, vol. I, p. 587, 591-594
138) Ewald, Diary, vol. III, p. 238 - 1780, Oct. 17
139) Ibid., vol. II, p. 97, 1776, Dec. 29
140) Ibid., vol. II, p. 55
141) Ibid., vol. II, p. 65
142) Schoepf, Johann David, *Reise*, p. VI
143) Bardeleben, *Deutsch-Amerikanische Geschichtsblaetter*, vol. XXVII-XXVIII
144) StAM 12.11. I Ba 10, p. 31
145) Ewald, Diary, vol. II, p. 187f.-1777, Aug. 25,26
146) Ibid., vol. IV, p. 12 f
147) Ibid., p. 186
148) Ibid., p. 239
149) Lith, Freiherr von der, *Feldzug der Hessen nach Amerika*, p. 19
150) *Briefwechsel meist historischen und politischen Inhalts* and *Stats-Anzeigen*
151) Schloezer, *Briefwechsel*, p. 149, Hinrichs to Schloezer, near Philadelphia, on the Neck, 1778, Jan. 18 (arrived at Goettingen 1778, Apr. 7)
152) Schubarth, Martin Christian Friedrich Daniel, *Deutsche Chronik*, 1777, Feb. 27
153) StAM 12.11. I Ba 2
154) Ibid., I Ba 13. p. 4-9
155) Ibid., 4h.409.3, 4h.411.3
156) LC, Ms. Hass. 8º42
157) NYPL, Hess. Ms., no. 26
158) Ibid., no. 33a, p. 301
159) Ibid., no. 21, 1776, Aug. 27
160) JP 1:16, 1776, Aug. 31-Sept. 4
161) Ibid., 1:55, In the camp near Philadelphia, 1777, Nov. 30
162) NYPL, Hess. Ms., no. 33a, p. 492
163) *Deutsch-Amerikanische Geschichtsblaetter*, vol. XXVII-XXVIII, p. 60
164) StAM 4h.412.3
165) Schloezer, I/5, p. 6, Savannah, 1779, Jan. 16
166) StAM, 12.11. I Ba 6, 1776, Dec. 8
167) Ibid., I Ba 17, p. 149, 159
168) Ewald, Diary, vol. II, p. 11
169) Ibid., vol. II, p. 174
170) Ibid., p. 182
171) Ibid., vol. III, p. 222f
172) StAM 12.11. I Ba 15, p. 72
173) Ibid., I Ba 16, p. 139
174) Schloezer, II/7, p. 13f
175) StAM 12.11. 1c
176) NYPL, Hess. Ms. no. 33a, p. 459, 461
177) Ewald, Diary, vol. I, p. 60f
178) JP 2:9, New York, 1778, July 7
179) Ewald, Diary, vol. IV, p. 142f
180) Ibid., vol. III, p. 100f
181) Ibid., vol. IV, p. 222
182) StAM 12.11. I Ba 12, 1782, July 20/21
183) Ewald, Diary, vol. IV, p. 318, 320
184) Faust, Albert Bernhardt, *The German Element in the United States*, vol. I, p. 296; Rosengarten, Joseph George, *The German Soldier in the Wars of the United States*, Phila., 1890, p. 100f
185) StAM 12.11. I Ba 2, 1776, Dec. 26
186) NYPL, Hess. Ms. no. 33a, p. 306
187) Ewald, Diary, vol. I, p. 242f
188) Schloezer, I/3, p. 259, Near Philadelphia, on the Neck, 1778, Jan. 18
189) NYPL, Hess. Ms. no. 27, p. 37
190) StAM 4h.410.1, New York, 1776, Dec. 22
191) JP 1:56, Baurmeister, near Philadelphia, 1777, Dec. 1
192) JP 4:2, New York, 1781, March 3 (the last page is a draft of a letter by von Jungkenn)

193) JP 6:35, Johann Jacob Fischer, New York, 1782, Dec. 17 (P. 4 is a draft of von Jungkenn's reply)
194) Moore, Frank, *Diary of the American Revolution*, vol. II, p. 176
195) Ewald, Diary, vol. I, p. 155-158
196) JP 3:38, New York, 1780, July 4
197) Ewald, Diary, vol. IV, p. 134f
198) Ibid., p. 254f
199) Ibid., p. 319f
200) StAM 12.11. I Ba 16, p. 300-306
201) NYPL, Hess. Ms., no. 26
202) Ibid., no. 12, 27
203) Ewald, Diary, vol. II, p. 45, 92f
204) Ibid., p. 141-145
205) Uhlendorf, *Siege of Charleston*, p. 158-159 note
206) Ewald, Diary, vol. III, p. 159f
207) Uhlendorf, *Siege of Charleston*, p. 157-159
208) NYPL, Hess. Ms. no. 33a, p. 293-295
209) Ibid., p. 380
210) StAM 12.11. I Ba 13, p. 52f
211) NYPL, Hess. Ms. no. 12, p. 46
212) StAM 4h.413.4, Extract of a letter of Lieutenant Henkelmann to secretary Strieder in Cassel, in the camp near Fort Knyphausen, 1777, Jan. 1
213) NYPL, Hess. Ms. no. 33a, p. 382f
214) JP 1:39, In the camp near Fort Knyphausen, 1777, July 5
215) NYPL, Hess. Ms. no. 26
216) StAM 12.11. I Ba 13, p. 52
217) Ibid., p. 81, 1777, June 24
218) Ibid., p. 54
219) Ibid., p. 76f
220) Ewald, Diary, vol. II, p. 6-8, Philadelphia, 1778, Jan. 30
221) JP 1:72, Philadelphia, 1778, May 10
222) StAM 12.11. I Ba 2, 1776, Dec. 26
223) *Hessenland* no. 24, 1906, p. 339f
224) StAM 4h.415.5., 1777, Oct. 16
225) *Hessenland* no. 24, 1906, p. 339
226) NYPL, Hess. Ms., no. 26
227) Moore, Frank, *Diary of the American Revolution*, vol. I, p. 233f
228) Bowman, Allan, *The Morale . . .*, p. 127, Annotation no. 72
229) Ewald, Diary, vol. II, p. 5f
230) *Deutsch-Amerikanische Geschichtsblaetter*, vol. XX-XXI, p. 259
231) NYPL, Hess. Ms. no. 12, 27
232) Ibid., no. 26
233) StAM 12.11. I Ba 13, p. 47f, 1776, Dec. 26
234) Schloezer, I/2, p. 100, New York, 1776, Sept. 18
235) StAM 4h.412.2. and StAM 12.11. I Ba 13, p. 47f
236) NYPL, Hess. Ms. no. 33a, p. 332
237) Ibid., p. 380
238) JP 2:33, New York, 1778, Nov. 16
239) *Letters of Members of the Continental Congress*, E.C. Burnett ed., vol. 2, p. 399
240) JP 2:61, Philadelphia, 1778, Jan. 20
241) Ewald, Diary, vol. II, p. 14
242) Schloezer, I/4, p. 166, On the Neck near Philadelphia, 1778, June 2
243) StAM 12.11. I Ba 13, p. 75
244) Schloezer, I/4, p. 116, On the Neck near Philadelphia, 1778, June 2
245) One Rhenish Florin was about a 25th of a thaler in the 18th century in Germany
246) Schloezer, I/9, p. 387, New York, 1780, Oct. 8
247) Ibid., I/4, p. 117
248) StAM 12.11. I Ba 18, p. 31f
249) Ewald, Diary, vol. I, p. 44
250) StAM 12.11. I Ba 9, p. 107f
251) Ibid., I Ba 18, p. 31f
252) Ibid., p. 36
253) StAM 4h.410.1, Headquarters, Long Island, 1776, Aug. 16
254) Ewald, Diary, vol. I., p. 70, 137, 162
255) Ibid., vol. II, p. 14; StAM 12.11. I Ba 4
256) StAM 4h.415, von der Malsburg to von Dittfurth, Charleston, 1781, July 1; Kuemmel, Heinrich, Field-chaplain, Journal, p. 91; Letter to Lt. Bauer, *Hessenland*, no. 24, 1906, p. 339
257) *New Jersey Journal*, 1780, July 12
258) JP 5:37, Mac Gowans Pass on York Island, 1782, Mar. 22
259) StAM 4h. 411.1 and StAM 12.11. I Ba 13, p. 110
260) JP 3:42, Friedrich von Hachenberg, New York, 1780, Aug. 12
261) Ewald, Diary, vol. IV, p. 357
262) Ensign Kleinschmidt of the Regiment von Woellwarth and Ensign Fuehrer of the Regiment von Knyphausen. StAM 4h.328.152; Lieutenant General von Knyphausen to the Landgrave, 1778, Aug. 24 — The returns of the Jaeger Corps list one officer as deserted but gives no name. StAM 12.1. 8853
263) Schloezer, I/3, p. 150, Near Philadelphia, on the Neck, 1778, Jan. 18
264) *Deutsch-Amerikanische Geschichtsblaetter*, vol. XX-XXI, p. 273
265) JP 1:61, Philadelphia, 1778, Jan. 20
266) JP 1:25, Newport, R.I., 1777, Jan. 8
267) Schloezer, I/3, p. 32, Rhode Island, 1777, June 24
268) JP 1:51, In the camp on Rhode Island, 1777, Nov. 8
269) JP 1:59, In the camp on Rhode Island, 1778, Jan. 6
270) JP 1:61, Philadelphia, 1778, Jan. 20
271) JP 1:67, Philadelphia, 1778, Apr. 12
272) JP 1:69, Philadelphia, 1778, Apr. 20
273) JP 2:38, Flushing, 1779, Jan. 7
274) JP 4:46, New York, 1781, July 15
275) Schloezer, I/2, p. 108
276) StAM 12.11. I Ba 13, p. 24
277) JP 3:38, New York, 1780, July 4
278) NYPL, Hess. Ms., no. 33a, p. 523
279) Schloezer, I/9, p. 384f, New York, 1780, Sept. 11
280) NYPL, Hess. Ms., no. 26
281) JP 2:2, Philadelphia, 1778, June 2
282) NYPL, Hess. Ms., 33b, p. 283ff
283) JP 6:48, New York, 1783, June 1
284) JP 5:47, Flushing, 1782, Mar. 7
285) JP 6:53, New York, 1783, Oct. 5

APPENDIX

HESSIAN LOSSES 1776-1784 (1)

	Died	Killed	Deserted	Captured	Dismissed
1776	445	71	66	1012	31
1777	1326	151	109	1020	21
1778	350	18	422	1229	40
1779	546	14	362	649	60
1780	692	29	288	621	24
1781	423	73	446	1508	80
1782	446	1	486	1182	31
1783	355	—	734	808	466
1784	43	—	36	—	161
Total	4626	357	2949	8029	914

(1) StA.M. 13. A 6, no. 23 p. 2

HESSIAN TABLE OF ORGANIZATION (1)

	OFFICERS	NON-COMS	SURGEONS	DRUMMERS	R & F
FIRST DIVISION					
Jaeger-company von Donop	4	12	1	3	105
Gren. Btl. von Linsing	16	44	4	20	420
Gren. Btl. von Block	16	44	4	20	420
Gren. Btl. von Minnigerode	16	44	4	20	420
Regt. de Corps	21	60	5	22	525
Regt. Prince Hereditary	21	60	5	22	525
Regt. Prince Carl	21	60	5	22	525
Regt. von Ditfurth	21	60	5	22	525
Regt. von Donop	21	60	5	22	525
Regt. (Old) von Lossberg	21	60	5	22	525
Regt. von Knyphausen	21	60	5	22	525
Regt. von Truembach	21	60	5	22	525
Regt. vacant Rall	21	60	5	22	525
Total	262	744	63	285	6615
SECOND DIVISION					
Jaeger-company Ewald	4	12	1	3	105
Artillery-company	5	14	1	3	129
Gren. Btl. Kochler	16	44	4	20	420
Regt. Landgrave	21	60	5	22	525
Regt. von Stein	21	60	5	22	525
Regt. von Wissenbach	21	60	5	22	525
Regt. von Huyne	21	60	5	22	525
Regt. von Buenau	21	60	5	22	525
Total	130	370	31	136	3279
Grand Total	392	1114	94	419	9894

(1) This indicates desired strength, not actual strength; StA.M. 13 A 6. no. 206

ORDERS OF BATTLE

ORDER OF BATTLE OF THE HESSIAN TROOPS 1776 (1)

Lt. Gen. von Heister
Lt. Gen. von Heister

Major Gen. von Mirbach	Major Gen. Stirn
Gren.-batl. Block	Gren.-batl. von Linsing
Regt. von Mirbach	Regt. de Corps
Regt. von Donop	Regt. Prince Carl
Regt. von Wutgenau	Regt. von Ditfurth
Regt. Prince Hereditary	Regt. Truembach

Lt. Gen. von Knyphausen

Colonel von Lossberg	Major Gen. Schmidt
Gren.-batl. Koehler	Gren.-batl. von Minnigerode
Regt. von Huyne	Regt. von Lossberg
Regt. von Stein	Regt. Rall
Regt. von Knyphausen	Regt. von Buenau

(1) StA.M. 409.3., p. 3f.

ORDER OF BATTLE FOR THE 1ST. HESSIAN DIVISION SINCE FEBR. 3, 1776 (1)

Lt. Gen. von Heister
Lt. Gen. von Heister

Major Gen. von Mirbach	Major Gen. Stirn
Regt. von Mirbach	Regt. de Corps
Regt. von Donop	Regt. Prince Carl
Regt. von Wutgenau	Regt. von Ditfurth
Regt. Prince Hereditary	Regt. von Truembach
Gren.-batl. Block	Gren.-batl. von Linsing

Lt. Gen. von Knyphausen

Colonel von Lossberg	Major Gen. Schmidt
Regt. von Huyne	Regt. von Buenau
Regt. von Stein	Regt. von Wissenbach
Regt. von Knyphausen	Regt. Rall
Gren.-batl. Koehler	Regt. (old) von Lossberg
	Gren.-batl. von Minnigerode

(1) StA.M. 13.A6, no. 237

ORDER OF BATTLE SINCE 1776, NOV. 27 (1)

Lt. Gen. von Heister
Lt. Gen. von Heister

Major Gen. von Mirbach	Major Gen. Stirn
Regt. v. Mirbach	Regt. de Corps
Regt. v. Donop	Regt. Prince Hereditary
Regt. Prince Carl	Regt. v. Ditfurth
Regt. Landgrave	Regt. v. Truembach
Gren.-batl. v. Minnigerode	Gren.-batl. v. Linsing

Lt. Gen. von Knyphausen

Colonel von Lossberg	Major Gen. Schmidt
Regt. v. Huyne	Regt. (old) v. Lossberg
Regt. v. Stein	Regt. Rall
Regt. v. Knyphausen	Regt. v. Wissenbach
Gren.-batl. Koehler	Regt. v. Buenau
	Gren.-batl. v. Lengercke

(1) StA.M. 13.A6, no. 237

ORDER OF BATTLE SINCE 1777, AUGUST 23 (1)

Lt. Gen. von Knyphausen

Major Gen. Schmidt	Major Gen. von Bose
Regt. Prince Carl	Regt. v. Truembach
Regt. Landgrave	Regt. v. Mirbach
Gren.-batl. v. Lengercke	Regt. v. Donop

Major Gen. Stirn	Major Gen. von Huyne
Regt. de Corps	Regt. v. Huyne
Regt. Prince Hereditary	Regt. v. Stein
Regt. v. Ditfurth	Regt. v. Knyphausen
Gren.-batl. v. Linsing	Gren.-batl. Koehler

Major Gen. von Lossberg

Regt. (Old) v. Lossberg
Regt. v. Woellwarth
Regt. v. Wissenbach
Regt. v. Buenau
Gren.-batl. v. Minnigerode

(1) StA.M. 13.A.6. 237

LAST ORDER OF BATTLE (EMBARKATION ORDER) (1)

Lt. Gen. von Lossberg
Lt. Gen. von Lossberg

Major Gen. von Hachenberg	Major Gen. von Kospoth
Major Gen. von Loos	Major Gen. von Wurmb

Regt. (Jung) v. Lossberg
Regt. v. Bose
Regt. Prince Carl
Regt. Prince Friedrich
Gren. batl. v. Lengercke

Jaeger-Corps
Regt. de Corps
Regt. Prince Hereditary
Regt. v. Donop
Regt. v. Ditfurth
Gren.-batl. v. Linsing

Lt. Gen. von Bose

Major Gen. von Gosen

Regt. v. Seitz
Regt. v. Benning
Regt. v. Porbeck
Regt. v. Knyphausen
Gren.-batl. Platte

Major Gen. von Knoblauch

Regt. (old) v. Lossberg
Regt. d'Angelleli
Regt. v. Knoblauch
Regt. v. Buenau
Gren.-batl. v. Loewenstein

(1) StA.M. 4h. 411. 3, p. 144

CHANGES OF NAMES OF HESSIAN UNITS 1776-1783 (1)

1. *Grenadier-Battalion von Linsing*
   1776: Grenadier-Battalion von Linsing
   Unchanged till 1783
2. *Grenadier-Battalion Block*
   1776: Grenadier-Battalion Block
   1777: Grenadier-Battalion von Lengercke
3. *Grenadier-Battalion von Minnigerode*
   1776: Grenadier-Battalion von Minnigerode
   1780: vacant
   1781: Grenadier-Battalion von Loewenstein
4. *Grenadier-Battalion Koehler*
   1776: Grenadier-Battalion Koehler
   1779: Grenadier-Battalion Graff
   1783: Grenadier-Battalion Platte
5. *Infantry-Regiment de Corps (Leib-Regiment)*
   1776: Leib-Regiment
   Unchanged till 1783
6. *Fusilier-Regiment Prince Hereditary (Regiment Erbprinz)*
   1776: Regiment Erbprinz
   Unchanged till 1783
7. *Infantry-Regiment Prince Carl (Regiment Prinz Karl)*
   1776: Regiment Prinz Karl
   Unchanged till 1783
8. *Infantry-Regiment von Wutgenau*
   1776: Regiment von Wutgenau
   1776: Regiment Landgrave (Landgraf)
9. *Fusilier-Regiment von Ditfurth*
   1776: Regiment von Ditfurth
   Unchanged till 1783
10. *Infantry-Regiment von Donop*
    1776: Regiment von Donop
    Unchanged till 1783
11. *Infantry-Regiment (Old) von Lossberg*
    1776: Regiment von Lossberg
    1777: Combined Regiment with Regts.
    Rall and von Knyphausen
    1777: Regiment (Old) von Lossberg
12. *Fusilier-Regiment von Knyphausen*
    1776: Regiment von Knyphausen
    1777: Combined Regt. with Regts.
    Rall and von Lossberg
    1777: Regiment von Knyphausen
13. *Grenadier-Regiment Rall*
    1776: Regiment Rall
    1777: Combined Regt. with Regts.
    von Lossberg and von Knyphausen
    1777: Regiment von Woellwarth
    1780: vacant von Truembach
    1781: Regiment d'Angelleli
14. *Infantry-Regiment von Mirbach*
    1776: Regiment von Mirbach
    1777: Regiment von Truembach
    1779: Regiment von Bose
15. *Infantry-Regiment von Truembach*
    1776: Regiment von Truembach
    1777: Regiment von Mirbach
    1782: Regiment (Jung) von Lossberg
16. *Infantry-Regiment von Stein*
    1776: Regiment von Stein
    1779: Regiment von Seitz
    1781: Regiment vacant von Huyne
    1782: Regiment von Seitz
    1783: Regiment von Knoblauch
17. *Infantry-Regiment von Wissenbach*
    1776: Regiment von Wissenbach
    1781: Regiment von Knoblauch
    1782: Regiment von Knoblauch
    1783: Regiment von Seitz
18. *Infantry-Regiment von Huyne*
    1776: Regiment von Huyne
    1781: Regiment von Knoblauch
    1782: Regiment von Benning
19. *Infantry-Regiment von Buenau*
    1776: Regiment von Buenau
    Unchanged till 1783

(1) StA.M. 13 A 6, No 232; The change of names was caused by the change of the Honorary Commanders, not by the change of Field-Commanders. Such an Honorary Command was not only a position of symbolic character but of actual significance for the ranking of this Commander in the military hierarchy of the Hessian Army. Naming of Honorary Commanders was common in German Armies till the end of the First World War.

RANK LIST OF HESSIAN OFFICERS 1777 (1)

INFANTRY REGIMENT DE CORPS

Commander
  Friedrich Wilhelm von LOSSBERG
Colonel
  Friedrich Wilhelm von WURMB
Lieutenant Colonel
  Otto Christian Wilhelm von LINSING
Major
  Hans Henrich Georg Wilhelm von BIESENRODT
Captains
  Lud[wig] Fried[rich] von STANFORTH
  Peter Michael WALDENBERGER
Staff Captains
  August von DINCKLAGE
  Carl Reinhard MOTZ
  Christian Matthias le LONG
  Melchior Friedrich von MILCKAU
  Friedrich Ernst von MUENCHHAUSEN
  Christian Friedrich von URFF
First Lieutenants
  Conrad DUPUY
  Fried[rich] Henrich von GRONING
  Henrich HEGEMANN
  Johann Martin MELTZHEIMER
Second Lieutenants
  Christoph BODE
  August Wilhelm von ENDE
  Justus Henrich ERNST
  Christoph Friedrich Julius KADEN
  Carl August KLEINSCHMIDT
  Caspar von GROENING
Cadets
  Peter LUDEMANN
  Johann Anton GERMER
  Bernhard Wilhelm WIEDERHOLD

FUSILIER REGIMENT PRINCE HEREDITARY

Commander
  Major General Johann Daniel STIRN
Colonel
  Carl Wilhelm von HACHENBERG
Lieutenant Colonel
  Johann Ludwig von COCHENHAUSEN
Major
  Matthias von FUCHS
Captains
  Henrich Friedrich WACHS
  [Ludwig] WINCKELMANN
    as of the 4th of April 1777 deceased
Staff Captains
  Ludwig Friedrich von GALL
  Henrich Sebastian von SCHALLERN
  Christoph LAUEN
  Johann Caspar KUEMMEL
First Lieutenants
  Herman Christoph GEBHARD
  Adolph von ESCHWEGE
Second Lieutenants
  Joachim KIMM
  Friedrich Wilhelm von HALLER
  Ernst Wolff BRIEDE
  Louis DESCOUDRES
  Ernst Friedrich von WESTERHAGEN
  Carl von OFFENBACH
  Wilhelm von ANDERSON
  Carl Wilhelm Friedrich GRAU
  Carl von BOYNEBURGK
Cadets
  Friedrich von KEUDEL
  Reinhard Friedrich UNGEWITTER
  Jacob Dietrich PFAFF
  Georg Ludwig MOTZ

INFANTRY REGIMENT PRINCE CARL

Commander
  Major General Martin Conrad SCHMITT
Colonel
  Johann Wilhelm SCHREIBER
Lieutenant Colonels
  Georg Emanuel von LENGERCKE
  Wilhelm von LOEWENSTEIN
Major
  Carl August von KUTZLEBEN
Captain
  Philipp von WURMB
Staff Captains
  Wilhelm von WILMOWSKY
  Jacob FISCHER
  Henrich Wilhelm REUTING
  Friedrich Adolph NEUBER
First Lieutenants
  Johann August GERSTMANN
  Theodor Hartmann HARTERT
  Balthasar SPANGENBERG
  Martin BECKER
Second Lieutenants
  Carl Georg von TROTT
  Johann von WESTPHALEN
  Wilhelm Carl Ludwig von GEYSOW
  Johann Philipp SCHMITT
  Ludwig Otto Carl von DOERNBERG
  Carl Wilhelm von TROTT
  Henrich SCHMITT
Cadets
  Barthold KNOLL
  Friedrich Adolph BECKER
  [von TROTT]
  Philipp Peter SCHMITT

INFANTRY REGIMENT LANDGRAVE

Colonel and Commander
  Carl von BOSE,
    made commandant as of the 7th May 1777
  Heinrich Julius von KOSBOTH, Colonel
Lieutenant Colonel
  Carl Christian von ROMRODT
Majors
  Caspar Friedrich von HANSTEIN
  Carl Gottlieb von ARENBERG
Captain
  Friedrich von ESCHWEGE
Staff Captains
  Johann Rudolph MONDORFF
  Johann Henrich HOHLEFELD
  Johann Jacob VOGT
First Lieutenants
  Johann Adam BAUER
  Adolph von ESCHWEGE
  Ludwig Eberhard MURARIUS
  Johann Conrad ERNST
  Peter VOLPERT
  August von KOSBOT
Second Lieutenants
  Ludwig von KOSBOTH
  Leopold Friedrich BERTOD
  Carl GOEDDAEUS
  Carl Joseph JULIAT
  Franciscus Hartmann von ENDE
Cadets
  Carl von SELHORST
  [Friedrich] von KOSBOTH
  Carl von BILSINGSLOEBEN
  Philipp WAGNER
  Adolph Friedrich Philipp von ZANTHIER

FUSILIER REGIMENT VON DITFOURTH

Commander
  Carl von BOSE
  Max von WESTERNHAGEN,
    transferred 8th May 1777 by the Landgrave as Commandant
Lieutenant Colonel
  Ferdinand Henrich von SCHULER
Major
  Leopold von BORCK
Captains
  Hermann Carl Christoph HENDORFF
  Friedrich von der MALSBURG
Staff Captains
  Nicolaus Friedrich KLINGENDER
  Philipp Ludwig REICHEL
  Ludwig EGGERDING
  Johannes WAGENER
First Lieutenants
  Wilhelm von der MALSBURG
  Henrich Hugo SCHEFFER
Second Lieutenants
  Georg Ernst TOEPFER
  Wilhelm Franz von DITFOURTH
  Arnold Wilhelm von HALLER
  Carl Friedrich von NORDECK zu RABENAU

Carl Levin MARQUARD
Leonhard Wilhelm von TRUMBACH
Carl Christian August von BOSE
Franz Ferdinand von BARDELEBEN
Adolph Friedrich DUNCKER
Cadets
  Georg Hermann VUTTEJUS
  Peter Christian FIRNHABER
  Henrich Anton SCHACHTEN
  Anton STRASSER

INFANTRY REGIMENT VON DONOP

Colonel
  David Ephraim von GOSEN
Lieutenant Colonels
  Carl Philipp HEYMEL
  Erasmus Ernst HINTHE
Majors
  Christian Moritz von KUTZLEBEN
  Carl von WURMB
Staff Captains
  Philipp Wilhelm von GALL
  Jean Matthé GISSOT
  Justus Friedrich VENATER
  Christoph Dietrich von DONOP
  Friedrich Wilhelm GEISTER
First Lieutenants
  Philipp Henrich MURHARD
  Emanuel Rosinus HAUSMANN
Second Lieutenants
  Johann Philipp REIS
  Carl Friedrich von NAGEL
  Henrich Ludwig von NAGEL
  Joh[ann] Henrich von BARDELEBEN
  Wilhelm von LEPEL
  Wilhelm Carl von DONOP
  Carl August FREYENHAGEN
  Jeremias von LOSSBERG
Cadets
  Eitel von TROTT
  Wilh[elm] Johann Ernst FREYENHAGEN
  Carl von KNOBLAUCH
  Friedrich MURHARD

INFANTRY REGIMENT VON LOSSBERG

Commander and Colonel
  Johann August von LOOS
Lieutenant Colonel
  Franciscus SCHEFFER
Major
  Ludwig August von HANSTEIN
Captains
  Ernst Eberhard von ALTENBOCKUM
  [Johann] Caspar REITZ,
    shot dead the 26th December 1776
Staff Captains
  [Friedrich] Wilhelm von BENNING,
    shot dead the 26th December 1776
  Adam Christoph STEDING
  Constantin von WURMB
First Lieutenants
  Friedrich Wilhelm KRAFFT
  [Georg] Christoph KIMM,
    shot dead the 26th December 1776
  Georg Wilhelm HILLE
Second Lieutenants
  Ludwig Wilhelm KELLER
  Ernst Christian SCHWABE
  Ernst Wilhelm von WINTZINGERODE
  Jacob PIEL
  Hermann Henrich Georg ZOLL
  Wilhelm Christian MOELLER
  Christian August von HOBEN
  Henrich Reinhard HILLE
  Ludwig von GLUER
Cadets
  Franz Friedrich GREBE
  Henrich Carl von ZENGEN
  Friedrich Christoph HENDORFF
  Christian von WALDSCHMIDT
  Georg Henrich KRESS
  Johann Henrich RATHMANN
  Ernst Christian von HOENNINGEN

FUSILIER REGIMENT VON KNYPHAUSEN

Honorary Commander
  Lieutenant General [Wilhelm] von KNYPHAUSEN
Commander
  Colonel Henrich von BORCK
Lieutenant Colonel
  Friedrich Ludwig von MINNIGERODE
Majors
  [Carl] Friedrich von DECHOW,
    wounded the 31st January 1777
  Joh[ann] Friedrich von STEIN
Captain
  Georg Wilhelm von BIESENRODT
Staff Captains
  Ludwig Wilhelm von LOEWENSTEIN
  Berthold Helfrich SCHIMMELPFENNIG
  Jacob BAUM
First Lieutenants
  Christoph Philipp REUFFURTH
  Andreas WIEDERHOLD
  Joh[ann] Nicolaus VAUPEL
  Henrich Friedrich ZINCK
Second Lieutenants
  Christian SOBBE
  Joh[ann] Friedr[ich] Wilhelm BRIEDE
  Wilhelm Ludwig von ROMRODT
  Joachim Hieronymus von BASSEWITZ
  Ernst Philipp Wilhelm HEYMEL
  Carl Ernst FUEHRER
  Werner von FERRY
  Ludwig Ferdinand von GEYSOW
Cadets
  Carl Friedrich FUEHRER
  Anthon Adolph August von LUTZOW
  Wilhelm von DRACH
  Henrich Christoph ZIMMERMAN
  Henrich RITTER

GRENADIER REGIMENT VON WOELWARTH

Honorary Commander
  Colonel Wolfgang Friedrich von WOELWARTH
Lieutenant Colonels
  Johann Christoph KOEHLER
  Balthasar BRETHAUER
Major
  Johann Jost MATTHAEUS
Captains
  Henrich Ludwig BOECKING
  Friedrich Wilhelm BODE
Staff Captains
  Johann Otto GOEBEL
  Joh[ann] Henrich BRUEBACH (dead)
  Friedrich Michael FEETZ
  Joh[ann] Henrich STERNICKEL
First Lieutenants
  Wilhelm Engelhard BRAUMANN
  Gregorius SALTZMANN
  Johannes STEBEL
Second Lieutenants
  Philipp Henrich WIDDEKIND
  Friedrich von GRIESHEIM
  Johann Christoph MUELHAUSEN
  Carl von DALLWIGK
  Wilhelm STUDENROTH
  Carl Andreas KINEN
  Ludwig KINEN
Cadets
  Johann Ludwig WERNICK
  Lebrecht FLECK
  Carl Wilh[elm] KLEINSCHMIDT
  Joh[ann] Georg SCHROEDER
  Joh[ann] Jacob WERNER
  Georg BROESCKE

INFANTRY REGIMENT VON MIRBACH

Honorary Commander
  Major General Werner von MIRBACH
Commander
  Colonel Justus Henrich BLOCK
Lieutenant Colonel
  Ernst Rudolph von SCHIECK
Majors
  Emanuel Anselm von WILMOWSKY
  Carl Leopold BAUERMEISTER
Captain
  Louis Marie de MALET
Staff Captains
  Johann Wilhelm ENDEMANN
  David REICHOLD
  Wilhelm Erdmann von BOJATSKY
  Johann Melchior ROTH
First Lieutenants
  Friedrich Andreas SCHOTTEN
  Conrad RIEMANN
  Johann Rudolph RODEMANN
Second Lieutenants
  Carl von WURMB
  Carl Henrich von TOLL
  Dietrich von GOTTSCHALL
  Friedrich August BROESCKE
  Johann Conrad SCHRAIDT
  Ludwig Wilhelm August von BOYNEBURGK
  Carl Friedrich RIEFFER
Cadets
  Georg WIESENMUELLER
  Hans Friedrich von BIESENRODT
  Carl Wilhelm von BILSINGSLOEBEN
  Erhard von DRACH
  Hieronymus BERNER

INFANTRY REGIMENT VON TRUEMBACH

Honorary Commander
  Major General von TRUEMBACH
Colonel
  Carl Ernst von BISCHHAUSEN
Lieutenant Colonel
  Borries Hilmar von MUENCHHAUSEN
Major
  Johann Christian DUBUY [DUPUY?]
Captains
  Maximilian Wilhelm von OREILLY
  Friedrich Henrich SCHEERER
Staff Captains
  Alexander von WILMOWSKY
  Moritz Christian von STEIN
  Johann Georg EIGENBROD
First Lieutenants
  Hermann Christian ROLL
  Wilhelm von LELIVA
  Friedrich Theodor SPENER
  Johann Jacob SCHWANER
Second Lieutenants
  Johann Philipp BUTTE
  Georg Christoph HOEPFNER
  Johann Josias GEISE
  Ludwig Wilhelm HENEL
  Franz Christoph HARTMANN
  Joseph von NETZER
  Theodor Friedrich Treusch von BUTLAR
Cadets
  [Christian] Friedrich August CLEVE,
    stabbed in a duel the 19th February 1777
  Johann Friedrich von KUNTZSCH
  Carl Wilhelm von BURGHOF
  Wilhelm von HORN
  Philipp Ernst von TROTT

INFANTRY REGIMENT VON STEIN

Colonel
  Franz Erdmann Carl von SEITZ
Lieutenant Colonel
  Arnold SCHLEMMER
Major
  Carl Wilhelm GRAFF
Captains
  Friedrich PLATTE
  Johannes NEUMANN
Staff Captains
  Johann Christoph von ENDE
  Johann Georg LANGENSCHWARTZ
  Andreas SANDROCK
  Wilhelm BODE
First Lieutenants
  Carl von ROMRODT
  Christian Jacob MUENCH
  Peter BRUEBACH
  Johann Erich VILMAR
  Wilhelm JUSTI
Second Lieutenants
  Andreas OELHANS
  Johann Henrich HENCKELMANN
  Engelbrecht von FREYDEN
  Arnold von LAHRBUSCH
  Johannes KNIES
Cadets
  Bernhard STUNZ
  Georg ALBUS
  Georg Henrich FENNER
  Reinhard JUNGK
  Adolph Christoph VIETH

INFANTRY REGIMENT VON WISSENBACH

Lieutenant Colonels
  Friedrich PORBECK
  Carl von KITZEL
Major
  Johann Georg SEELIG

Captains
  Georg HOHENSTEIN
  Johannes GUNDERMANN
Staff Captains
  Georg STEBEL
  Jacob BODICKER
  Joh[ann] Jacob OSWALD
First Lieutenants
  [Johann] Jacob SCHEFFER,
    died the 24th February 1777
  Henrich Christoph GERMER
  Friedrich Wilhelm HUEPEDEN
  Wilhelm Ludwig Henrich HEEGEMANN
  Johann Anton von DALWIGK
  Philipp ROESING
Second Lieutenants
  Jeremias LOTZ
  Conrad KOERBER
  Wilhelm STIPPICH
  Samuel WALDECK
  Christoph GOEBEL
  Christian BEERMANN
Cadets
  Ludwig ERNST,
    died the 18th February 1777
  Johann Ludwig KLEYENSTEUBER
  Georg SCHENCK
  Johann Christoph KOERBER

INFANTRY REGIMENT VON HUYNE

Honorary Commander
  Colonel Johann Christoph von HUYNE
Lieutenant Colonel
  Hubert Frantz KURTZ
Majors
  Johann Philipp HILDEBRAND
  Melchior MARTINI
Captain
  Johann Friedrich Zacharias WAGNER,
    died the 11th March 1777
Staff Captains
  Georg Friedrich von SCHALLERN
  Johann Henrich SONNEBORN
  Reinhold HEILEMANN
First Lieutenants
  Carl WEGENER
  Dietrich REINHARD
  Claudius STUECK
Second Lieutenants
  Johannes HOECKER
  Jeremias ROEPENACK
  Franz Adam KUHL
  Johannes KRUPP
  Friedrich STARCKLOFF
  Friedrich Wilhelm WENDT
Cadets
  Georg Bernhard KERSTING
  Rudolph Wilhelm DUNCKER
  Martin Ludwig WISCKER
  Ludwig GRAU

INFANTRY REGIMENT VON BUENAU

Colonel and Honorary Commander
  Rudolph von BUENAU
Lieutenant Colonel
  Johann Adam SCHEFFER
Majors
  Wilhelm Eckard MATTHIAS
  Philipp Christian HELL
Captains
  Johann Christoph STUDENROTH
  Henrich Christian HESSENMUELLER
Staff Captains
  Johann Christian GOEBEL
  Philipp Christian FIRNHABER
  Johann Ernst FERRAND
  August Christian NOLTENIUS
First Lieutenants
  Johann Bartholomaeus BECKER
  Johann Jacob FRITSCH
  Johann Christoph FELDNER
  Johannes WIEGAND,
    died the 12th February 1777
Second Lieutenants
  Balthasar MERTZ
  Johann Andreas BORNEMANN
  Christian Otto FROHN
  Ernst von HARSTALL
  Johann Henrich BRAUNS
  Philipp Ferdinand Wolff von GUDENBERG
  Henrich BAUER

Cadets
  Christian Ernst KLEYENSTEUBER
  Friedrich GAMBERT
  Georg LYNCKER
  Joh[ann] Henrich BODE

FIELD JAEGER CORPS

Commander
  Colonel Carl [Emil] von DONOP
Lieutenant Colonel
  Ludwig Johann Adolph von WURMB
Major
  Ernst Carl von PRUESCHENCK
Captains and Captains of Cavalry
  Johannes EWALD
  August von WREEDEN
  Friedrich Henrich LOHREY
Staff Captains and Captains of Cavalry
  [Friedrich] Wilhelm von GROTHAUSEN,
    died the 9th January 1777
  Fried[rich] Wilhelm von DONOP,
    died the 6th February [ ]
  Joh[ann] and Fried[rich] Jacob TRAUTWETTER
First Lieutenants
  Franz Christian von BODUNGEN
  Georg Hermann HEPPE
  Carl von RAU
  Carl Moritz von DONOP
  [Johann] HINRICHS
  Friedrich Adam Julius von WANGENHEIM
Second Lieutenants
  Johann Wilhelm von HAGEN, senior
  Erich Carl von HAGEN, junior
  Friedrich KELLERHAUS
  Johann Henrich WOLFF
  Francois Joseph de MESY
  Louis de Montluisant de FOIGNY
  Johannes SCHEFFER

GRENADIER BATTALION VON LINSING (2), (3)

Lieutenant Colonel and Commander
  [Otto Christian] von Linsing

Captains	Transferred from
Von Wurmb	3rd Batt. Guards
Von Eschwege	2nd Batt. Guards
Von Stanford	Regt. de Corps
Von Malet	Regt. von Mirbach
Staff Captain	
Von Westerhagen	2nd Batt. Guards
First Lieutenants	
Von Eschwege	3rd Batt. Guards
Dupuy	Regt. de Corps
Von Groening	2nd Batt. Guards
Second Lieutenants	
Rothe (Adjutant)	Regt. von Mirbach
Rodemann	Regt. von Mirbach
Von Groening	Regt. de Corps
Von Brumbach	3rd Batt. Guards
Waitz von Eschen	3rd Batt. Guards
Von Ende	Regt. de Corps
Von Westerhagen	2nd Batt. Guards
Von Gottschall	Regt. von Mirbach

Quartermaster
  Broeske
Surgeon
  George
Provost
  Augenstein

GRENADIER BATTALION KOEHLER (4)

Lieutenant Colonel and Commander
  [Johann Christoph von] Koehler

Captains	Transferred from
Heinrich Christian Hessenmueller	Von Buenau
Johann Neumann	Von Stein
Friedrich Wilhelm Bode	Rall
Georg Hohenstein	Von Wissenbach
Staff Captain	
Jacob Wilhelm Bode	Von Stein
First Lieutenants	
Christoph Ludwig von Romrod	Von Stein
Friedrich Wilhelm Huepeden	Von Wissenbach
Johann Jacob Fritsch	Von Buenau
Balthasar Mertz	Von Buenau
August Friedrich von Linghersdorf	Rall
Johann Anton von Dalwigk	Von Wissenbach
Second Lieutenants	
Carl von Dalwigk	Rall
Andreas Oehlhaus	Von Stein
Wilhelm Studenroth	Rall
Wilhelm Stippich	Von Wissenbach
Johann Henrich Brauns (adjutant)	Von Buenau

GRENADIER BATTALION VON MINNIGERODE (5)

Lieutenant Colonel and Commander
  Friedrich Ludwig Christoph von Minnigerode

Captains	Transferred from
Herman Hendorff	Von Ditfurth
Friedrich Wachs	Prince Hereditary
Friedrich Ernst von Muenchhausen	Von Lossberg
Berthold Helferich Schimelpfenig	Von Knyphausen
Constantin von Wurmb	Von Lossberg
Emanuel Wagner	Von Ditfurth
First Lieutenants	
Friedrich Zinck	Von Knyphausen
Herman Gebhard (adjutant)	Prince Hereditary
Second Lieutenants	
Georg Doyser	Von Ditfurth
Wilhelm von Wintzingerode	Von Lossberg
Friedrich von Haller	Prince Hereditary
Carl von Rabenau	Von Ditfurth
Wilhelm Heimell	Von Knyphausen
Ludwig von Geyso	Von Knyphausen
Henrich Hille	Von Lossberg

GRENADIER BATTALION VON LENGERKE (6)

Colonel and Commander
  Georg Emanuel von Lengerke

	Transferred from (7)
Major	
Wilhelm von Wilmowsky	Prince Carl
Captains	
Johann Mathias Gisset	Von Donop?
Georg Eichenbrodt	Truembach
Johann Friedrich Vogt	Landgrave?
Staff Captain	
Wilhelm Renting	Prince Carl?
First Lieutenants	
Philipp Reiss	Von Donop
Louis von Kospoth	Landgrave?
Carl Georg von Trott	Prince Carl
Wolf von Geyso	[ ]
Johann Friedrich von Kuntzsch (adjutant)	Truembach
Second Lieutenants	
Jeremias von Lossberg	Von Donop
Wilhelm von Trott	Prince Carl
Friedrich von Kospoth	Landgrave
Adolph Friedrich von Zanthier	Landgrave
Cadets	
Jacob Biskamp	[ ]
Carl Philipp von Kraft	Von Donop?

(1) Although undated, it is quite certain that this list (excluding grenadier battalions) was made during the summer of 1777. (StA.M. 11, no. 68, p. 1-37)
(2) At the outbreak of war, Carl Emil Ulrich von Donop was colonel of the 1st battalion of Guards and aide-de-camp to the Landgraff of Hesse-Cassel, Friedrich II. When the subsidiary treaties were negotiated with Great Britain, Colonel von Donop organized the Jaeger corps of hunters and marksmen and a brigade of grenadiers. The grenadier battalions were organized by detaching grenadier companies from existing regiments.
(3) StA.M. 12, 11, no. 556; list made summer of 1776; list does not mention the first names of the officers.
(4) StA.M. 12, 11, no. 554; list made summer of 1776.
(5) StA.M. 12, 11, no. 858; list made October 1777.
(6) StA.M. 12, 11, no. 8838; list made August 1783.
(7) No names of transfer from other units given in this list.

LIST OF HESSIAN PRISONERS WHO WENT OUT TO WORK AND THE NAMES OF THEIR EMPLOYERS (1) (2)

REGIMENT OF RALL

	NAME OF HESSIAN	*THEIR EMPLOYER*	*PLACE OF ABODE*
1.	HELLENBRAND, William	Christopher THURBER	Lebanon
2.	ANDRECHT, David	Henry MEYER	Lebanon
3.	OYFERT, Ernst		
4.	AMILONG, Henry	John WETZLER	Lebanon
5.	WALBERG, Christian	Benjamin MOORE	Lebanon
6.	STUDENROAD, Henry	Valentine KRUGH	Lancaster
7.	ANHORD, Verner	Peter KELLER	Lancaster
8.	ELGER, Jost		
9.	BRONBMEYER, Henry	George BURKHART	Lancaster
10.	TROUP, Adam		
11.	BRECHT, Jacob	Frederick MAN	do
12.	HEIKMAN, Christian	George CRYDER	do
13.	YOUNG, Christoph	Michael REINHARD	do
14.	POSSENHEIM, Ludwick		
15.	LONGENHAVEN, John	Jacob STEGER	Lebanon
16.	GERHALD, Gieve	Michael SWARTZ	
17.	MIDDAW, John	Nicholas ZOLLINGER	Heidelberg
18.	ZELTENSLAGER, Christian	Conrad MEYER	do
19.	KALTE, John	Henry MINCHEY	Lebanon
20.	HILLENBRAND, John		
21.	FOGAL, Justus	Adam ROTH	Lebanon
22.	GERSTEN, John		
23.	CARLE, Henry		
24.	KNOBEL, John		
25.	DEYENHARD, Henry	William BOWMAN Esqr.	Lancaster
26.	FLECK, George		
27.	WALDACK, Henry		
28.	KESSLER, Leo	Fredrick DORCIUS	Heidelberg T
29.	EIFER, Ernst	Henry MINCHEY	Lebanon
30.	SHENEWALT, Andreas	Henry ROWALT	Lebanon
31.	MILLER, Conrad	Rudolph KINSLEY	Tulpenhocken
32.	ROSE, Johannes	Matthias SLOUGH	Lancaster
33.	THONE, Martin	Henry HAIN	do
34.	MUMBERG, Dietrich	Philip Peter HOUTZ	Bethel T
35.	LEBER, George	Henry HOOK	Lancaster
36.	HENRY, Francis	Andreas WHY	Heidelberg T
37.	HOFF, Christoph	Christoph STASSER	Lebanon
38.	LOHR, Adam	Peter SWANGER	Heidelberg T
39.	BECHER, George	Jacob OYER	Lebanon T
40.	CANT, Ludwick		
41.	FISHER, Ludwick	Martin ERHART	Rapho T
42.	SHEFFER, Henry	Henry HINCKLE	do
43.	EBERT, Nicholas		
44.	BECKER, Helwig	Martin SPENGLER	Tulpenhocken
45.	KEPHEN, John		
46.	SIEBERT, Adam	George DOLLINGER	Bethel T
47.	GELTMACHER, Henry	John ALSPAUGH	Lancaster
48.	WAGNER, August Tyrius		
49.	MILLER, Henry	William BOWMAN Esqr.	Lancaster
50.	KUNRUMPF, Adam		
51.	WERNER, Conrad		

#	Name	Sponsor	Location
52.	ETTER, John	Andrew GRAFF	Lancaster
53.	GIESEL, George	William ROSS	do
54.	DEHN, Conrad	Anthony WELTY	do
55.	LOWFINK, John	Majr. Matthew SMITH	Paxton
56.	HEVELER, Paulus	Christopher AMALONG	Lebanon
57.	SMOLL, Andreas	Christian CAUFMAN or Stephen HORNBERGER	Manor T
58.	GISLER, Henry	Martin WEISER	Heidelberg
59.	STRUBE, Jacob		
60.	LAUTERBACH, John	Martin HEGEY	Warwick
61.	PEEPER, Henry		
62.	KETTING, Jacob	Jacob HAGEY	Warwick T
63.	VENUS, Henry	John REWALT	Lebanon
64.	SEGER, Henry	William CRAWFORD	Earl T
65.	GRAPPE, George	Casper EGLE	Lancaster
66.	HEIN, Herman	Frederick CAMPERT	Bethel T
67.	ASSMAN, Johann George	Philip HEVELFINGER	Tulpenhocken
68.	FEHRE, Henry	John TINGAS	Lebanon T
69.	ENGELHARD, John	Henry GEORGE	Lancaster
70.	FUHRER, John	Nicholas ENSMINGER	Cocalico
71.	GREBENDEICK, Henry	John STOSSER	Lebanon
72.	VENUS, Christoph	Christian SOWER	Tulpenhocken
73.	WEYMAN, Henry	Geo. Fredk. NAGLE	Lebanon
74.	BLUM, John Adam	Philip GLONINGER	do
75.	ROSS, John George	Jacob MYLEY	Bethel T
76.	JACOB, John George		
77.	HERBOLD, Henry	John SHWEITZER	do
78.	JEKEL, Henry		
79.	YOUNGERMAN, Henry	Sebastian GRAFF	Lancaster
80.	BERGE, Andreas	Philip HEVELFINGER	Tulpenhocken
81.	HALVERSTAD, Anthony	James LOW	Hanover
82.	BUTE, Corp. Jacob	Daniel NEFF	Hellam Township York County
83.	GROSSMAN, Henry		
84.	WIEDEKING, Henry		
85.	OTTO, Jacob		
86.	SHOUP, John		
87.	PETER, John	John WRIGHT	do
88.	WICK, Christoph	Capt. Casper STOEVER	Bethel T
89.	SHULTZ, John		
90.	DEMIES, John	George Adam STUMP	do
91.	HOUSMAN, Jacob	Valentine BENDER	Tulpenhocken
92.	HEINEMAN, Henry	Christopher KUCHER	Lebanon
93.	MANDER, Henry		
94.	BALL, John	Casper DOMAN	Bethel T
95.	ZILLICK, Henry	Mark BIRD Esqr.	Reading
96.	MILLER, John		
97.	KOCH, Jacob		
98.	DERKS, Martin	George ROSS, Jr.	Lancaster
99.	CLEVE, John Bernard		
100.	RICHTER, Conrad	Richd. LEMMON & Comp.	Baltimore Maryland
101.	STOCK, Corpl.	Col. Curtiss GRUBB	[Cornwall]

REGIMENT OF KNYPHAUSEN

#	Name	Sponsor	Location
1.	LINDEMAN, Henry	Capt. Philip WEISER	Lebanon
2.	GOSH, Justus	Christopher EMBRICK	do
3.	DERRINGER, Henry	David KROUSE	do
4.	YOUNG, Conrad	Philip FOUST	do
5.	GARKE, Henry	John PATTON	Berks Coty.
6.	DIEMAL, George		
7.	DIEMAL, Bastian		
8.	READING, Jost	Jacob HOFFMAN	Tulpenhocken
9.	OYL, Henry	Col. John ROGERS	Hanover
10.	KNOUF, Helwig	Henry SHEFFER Esqr.	Heidelberg
11.	FOGHT, Henry		
12.	LONG, Henry		
13.	WETZEL, Henry	Christopher EMBRICK	Lebanon
14.	EIGENBROD, William	Paul TUSSING	do
15.	SHEALEN, William	Michael MOSSER	Lancaster
16.	GRETE, Conrad		
17.	KERSHNER, Paul	George MOSSER	do
18.	STEIN, Jacob	Ludwig SHELL	do
19.	GREIR, John		
20.	LINDEMAN, Adam	John HUNTER	do
21.	LONG, John	Peter MILLER	do
22.	SHOT, Philip	Capt. Philip WEISER	Lebanon
23.	RED, Nicholas	Jacob PHILIPPY	Heidelberg
24.	REIMSHUSSEL, Christian	Peter GONTER	Lancaster
25.	BONSTEIN, Paul	David MILLER	Lancaster
26.	BONSTEIN, John	Richard HENRY	do
27.	SNYDER, Conrad	Col. Curtiss GRUBB	[Cornwall]
28.	SPIEGEN, John	Peter STEVEN	Lampeter
29.	KNINE, Conrad	Peter HEILMAN	Lanc.
30.	CORREL, Henry	Capt. Abraham FERRY	Rapho
31.	SHELLER, William	Nicholas BOOS	Lanc.
32.	MILFORT, John Jost	Col. John HUBER	Warwick
33.	BERTZ, John	Jacob KRUG	Lanc.
34.	HEIKENROAD, Justus	Peter HEILMAN	do
35.	KURTZ, Andreas	Matthias SLOUGH	do
36.	KOCK, John		
37.	ANSPACH, Henry	Sebastian GRAFF	do
38.	REIS, John		
39.	KELLER, Henry	Robert PATTON	Lebanon
40.	DIEL, Adam	Stephan MARTIN	Lanc.
41.	KELLER, John	Andrew LEVY	do
42.	SMITH, Conrad	Ludowick LOWMAN	do
43.	WILHELM, Henry		
44.	EILE, Nicholas	Saml. & Adam WILLHELM	near Lanc.
45.	SHEFFER, Henry		
46.	STERMAN, Herman	Saml. BOYD	Wrights Ferry
47.	CORREL, William		
48.	GEESE, John Jost		
49.	WAGNER, Conrad	Saml. WRIGHT	
50.	HASENPLUGH, Blasius	Charles KLUGH	Lanc.
51.	ENGELMOHR, Peter	Charles CANARY	do
52.	RUTHBERGER, Conrad	Francis BAILEY	do
53.	SHULTZ, Henry	Jas. CUNNINGHAM	Mountjoy
54.	STEINBREIHER, William	Bernard ZIMMERMAN	Hempfield
55.	TIPPEL, Henry Adam	Stephen HORNBERGAR	do
56.	SHWALM, John	Christian HARE	Mountjoy
57.	WEISMILLER, Henry		
58.	FENNER, Henry	David KROUSE	Lebanon
59.	LEINEWEBER, Henry	James CUNNINGHAM	Mountjoy
60.	BECKER, Henry	Nicholas LIEBRICH	Manheim
61.	KUNTZ, George	John PALMER	Cocalico T
62.	DEHN, Philip	His Excellency Thos. WHARTON Esqr.	
63.	DIEL, Conrad	Henry KRUM	Hanover T
64.	BATTENBERG, Henry	Dorothea PREESE	do
65.	MILLER, Nicholas Henry	Michael STROW	do
66.	BEGHTEL, John	John FURE	do
67.	KURTZ, Henry	Mr. James EWING	Hellam T
68.	DAMES, John Henry	Adam HARPER	Hanover T
69.	KURTZ, Henry		
70.	BECKERT, Henry	John JAMISON	Mountjoy
71.	HEINMILLER, Henry		
72.	WICKERT, John	Robert JAMISON	Londonderry T
73.	BLETTNER, Henry	Jacob COOK Esqr.	do
74.	HOUST, Henry	John ENGLISH	Womelsdorf Town
75.	DEIL, Nicholas	Christian SOWER	Tulpenhocken
76.	PETER, Henry	John STEIN	Heidelberg
77.	SHROCK, John	Henry KUPLINGER	Tulpenhocken
78.	HAMMER, Henry	Frederick HUBER	Bethel T
79.	GLEIBERT, Henry	Thomas HUMES	Hanover
80.	FISHER, Henry	Valentine GARDNER	Martick T
81.	GRAPP, John	Alexr. SCOTT	Hempfield
82.	FANNER, John	George SENEFF	Lanc.
83.	MUHL, Peter		
84.	HEER, Nicholas	Bernard GARDNER	Cocalico
85.	BATZ, John		
86.	SHEFER, Conrad	Wendal HIPSHMAN	Cocalico
87.	LERCH, Werner		
88.	DRANYENSTEIN, John	Abraham GRAFF	Cocalico
89.	WEIGAND, Henry		
90.	OX, Henry		
91.	HESS, Henry	George FLOCK	Warwick
92.	HECK, Nicholas	Robert CUNNINGHAM	Mountjoy
93.	STIPPEL, Adam	George STEWART	Hanover
94.	DIETZ, Conrad	Joseph FOLS	Heidelberg
95.	BIERWERT, Burkhart	Jacob SMITH	Tulpenhocken
96.	DIELMAN, Wiegard	Hynonimus HENTZELMAN	Manheim
97.	STORTZ, Laurence	Thomas ANDERSON	Donegal
98.	KEHLER, Henry	Michael MOORE	Heidelberg
99.	WIEGEL, Nicholas	John TEMPLETON	Hanover
100.	HINCKEL, Nicholas	Christopher KUCHER	Lebanon
101.	LIPPERT, Henry	Abraham DE BOY	Bethel
102.	MUNK, Adam	Jost LERCH	Heidelberg
103.	HAHN, George		
104.	GEBAUR, John	Christian FISHER	Tulpenhocken
105.	FOULHAVEN, Jost	Henry HOUSER	Tulp. B. Co.
106.	HEINMILLER, John	Christoph HENRY	Hanover
107.	ROTH, Peter	George ZELLER	Tulpenhocken
108.	EISENACH, Charles	John ECKERT	Heidelberg T B. Co.
109.	CORREL, Andreas	George COYER	Warwick
110.	DIETRICK, Justus	Timothy GOREN Esqr.	Hanover
111.	HEER, Henry	Col. John HUBER	Warwick
112.	KUNTZ, Conrad	John PALLMER	Cocalico
113.	ITZENHAUSER, John	George Nicholas LECHNER	Tulp.
114.	HOUPT, Christian		
115.	STUMP, John	Conrad ECKERT	Heidelberg
116.	DERR, Bastian	John BOWER	do
117.	HAPPEL, Valentine	Jno. MORRIS Esqr.	Lanc.
118.	HOMAN, Conrad	William HUNTER	Londonderry
119.	BECHTEL, John	Mark BIRD Esqr.	Reading
120.	KLIPPERT, Jacob		
121.	CLAUS, John		
122.	CORT, John Yost		
123.	HAPPEL, Conrad	Conrad FORCE	Lanc.
124.	SPOHR, Conrad	Daniel STAUFER	Lebanon

#	Name		Place
125.	SEYBEL, Corpl. Conrad	Ludwick WEAVER	Cocalico
126.	NISEL, Conrad	Richd. LEMON & Comp.	Baltimore
127.	ZIEGLER, George	Matthew IRWIN Esqr.	Reading
128.	SPENGLER, John		
129.	MARTIN, Jost		
130.	SHWALM, Henry		
131.	SHELMAN, Henry		
132.	SHNEIDER, John		

REGIMENT OF LOSBERG

#	Name		Place
1.	FELTMAN, Daniel		
2.	HANSING, John Gerhard		
3.	LANDIVER, Frederick	Christopher EMBERGH	Lebanon
4.	RINNER, Christian		
5.	BUCK, Henry		
6.	HINEMAN, Henry	Tawb GERMAN	do
7.	MENIKING, Henry	Sebastian WOLF	Bethel T
8.	RENSHELMAN, Frederick	Jacob HOFFMAN	do
9.	PRIESMYER, Henry	Nicholas ERHARD	Hanover
10.	FEGHTMEYER, Ludwick	John OFFNER	Lancaster
11.	WAGNER, Henry		
12.	NIEHOUSE, Henry	John GREINER	do
13.	MATTHIAS, Henry		
14.	BOLTE, Henry	Jacob ZANECK	do
15.	KOCH, Matthias		
16.	PFLIEGER, Simon	Peter KELLER	do
17.	HOSS, Ludwick		
18.	LEIB, Conrad	Francis BAILEY	do
19.	THAMER, Christopher	George BURKHART	do
20.	SHAWBER, Frederick	Martin DORWART	do
21.	BECKMAN, Joseph	William COOPER	do
22.	HARTMAN, Charles	Arnold BAMBERGER	do
23.	HEITOR, Christoph	Frederick MAN	do
24.	HOMEYER, Anthony	Daniel FRANK	do
25.	BLUM, Henry	John THOMA [ ]	Lebanon T
26.	STIMM, Dietrich		
27.	GUILTENPFENNIG, Doctr.	Capt. Danl. OLDENBRINK	Lebanon T
28.	HATTENDORF, Henry	Ludwick URBORN	Conestoga
29.	FAWBER, Frederick	William YOUNG	Hanover
30.	HUBER, Anthony	John FIELD	do
31.	BUCHMEYER, William	William YOUNG	do
32.	EPRECHT, Frederick	Andrea Adam LUTZ	Lancaster
33.	HUE, Gerhard	John REISHLING	do
34.	BRICKEL, John	Lawrence MARGENTLAND	do
35.	SMITH, Henry	Jacob LAUBSHER	Lebanon
36.	BEETE, Charles		
37.	MANTZ, Henry	William COOPER	Lancaster
38.	PAUL, John	At the Cont'l Stores under the direction of MR. SHALLEN	do
39.	SMITH, John		
40.	FEGHTMEYER, Henry	Col. MANTILLER	Lebanon
41.	SPILECKER, William	Henry REINAEL	do
42.	BODENSICK, Arnold	George KOCH	Lancaster
43.	MESMOCHER, Conrad	Paul LAHR	Bethel T
44.	WINTER, Ludwig	George PETER	Hanover
45.	MEYER, Conrad	Martin YENSAL	Lebanon
46.	HUCKSHOLD, Henry		
47.	ROLING, John Christian	Francis BAYLOR	do
48.	WHY, Anthony	John GREAM	Hanover
49.	NIEMAN, Frederick	Daniel BRODLEY	do
50.	KNEIF, Herman	John EMRICH	Bethel
51.	EICHOFF, Henry	Michael BROWN	Hanover
52.	FOGHT, Henry		
53.	TUNNERMAN, John	George DOLLINGER	Bethel
54.	OSTERMAN, Frederick	George MOORE	Lancaster
55.	WALBAUM, William		
56.	MEYER, Jacob	Jasper YEATES Esqr.	do
57.	PFINGSTEN, John Henry	Majr. Matthew SMITH	Paxton
58.	THOMAS, Henry	Saml. BOYD	Wrights Ferry
59.	LANDWEHR, Ludwick	Bernard ZIMMERMAN	Hempfield
60.	AKEMAN, Christoph	Archibald SLOAN	Hanover
61.	BIERMAN, Ludwig	Melchior RAHM	do
62.	MILLER, Herman Henry		
63.	WILLHOUSEN, Frederick	John STREHR	Lebanon
64.	FARRACAMP, Henry	Mr. Jas. EWING	Hallam T
65.	HATTENDORF, Henry		
66.	THLINGENBERG, Conrad	James JACKS	Manor T
67.	WILLHOUSEN, Ludwick		
68.	MEYER, Herman	Adam HERPER	Hanover
69.	WORTMAN, Henry	Isaac CRALL	Bethel
70.	BUNTER, Justus		
71.	REIGASS, Christoph	Michael MENNIG	Heidelberg
72.	ESHMAN, John Daniel	Stophel HEYAR	Lancaster
73.	NODBUSH, William	Nicholas ENSININGER	Cocalico
74.	WISSEL, William	Andrew BOWSMAN	Lancaster
75.	SOBAUM, Henry	Christian SOWER	Tulpenhocken
76.	KLINGENBERG, Frederick	George HOLSTEIN	Heidelberg
77.	NAGEL, Frederick	Leonard SWARTZ	Bethel
78.	HARDMAN, John Christoph	Martin STUP	Tulpenhocken
79.	STEGE, Hillmer	Jacob BRUNNER	Hanover
80.	BOLTE, Henry	George SENOFF	Lancaster
81.	VENUS, George		
82.	CAPMEYER, Herman		
83.	CALVEY, Ernst	Saml. BROADLEY	Londonderry
84.	HOLLING, Henry		
85.	WEIGE, Herman	Henry BRENDLE	Cocalico
86.	HARTWIG, Henry	George SENOFF	Lancaster
87.	LAUMAN, Frederick	Peter SPYCKER Esqr.	Tulpenhocken
88.	DEHN, Frederick	Peter ANSPACH	do
89.	GELLERMAN, Frederick	Henry EBERLE	Manor T
90.	SHMID, Henry		
91.	KNEIF, William		
92.	JACOB, Ernst		
93.	HUBY, Corpl. William	John BARKER	Rapho
94.	BEIGER, Henry	James ANDERSON	Donegal
95.	MILLER, Frederick	John BAILEY	do
96.	FREVERT, Conrad	James BAILEY	do
97.	SANDMAN, William	John ENGLE	Warwick
98.	ROSE, Corporal Herman	George MEILEY	Lebanon
99.	BUSSE, Otto		
100.	FELT, George	Michael ZELLER	Heidelberg
101.	HAMEYER, Frederick	John YOUNG	Hanover
102.	STARCK, John	Richard DARMOND	do
103.	GERRETZ, John	Francis ZERMAN	Lebanon
104.	SAAK, Moritz	Dr. Robt. HARRIS	Cape May N. Jersey
105.	PASSENBERG, Ludwick		
106.	DEYERBERG, Henry	George ROSS Junr.	Lancaster
107.	DOGAN, Frederick		
108.	SIEGMAN, Christoph		
109.	ZIMMERMAN, Henry	Richard LEMMON & Comp.	Baltimore
110.	GLOTZBACH, Matthias		Maryland
111.	MEYER, Christian		
112.	HOMUTH, Franic Henry		
113.	DEGENHARD, John	Mr. Robert PATTON	Lebanon

ARTILLERY

#	Name		Place
1.	HINCKEL, Henry	Jacob GERMAN	Lebanon T
2.	CERSLING, Justus	Col. Robert WHITE	Cumberland Co.
3.	KOHL, Henry	John Swigart IMBODEN	Lebanon
4.	GIESY, Matthius	Adam EDELMAN	Lancaster
5.	KREMER, Henry		
6.	EALING, Christoph	Michael GRUNDMACKER	do
7.	CRUMAN, Jost	Valentine KRUG	do
8.	SPRINGER, Jacob	William FLICK	do
9.	KNIPP, John	Adam ULRICH	do
10.	LEVRINGSHOUSEN, Christoph	Jacob DICKERT	do
11.	ANTING, Adam	Reinhard YOUNG	Lebanon T
12.	RIEMHOLD, Henry	Peter SMITH	Bethel T
13.	LUDENLUFF, Henry	Michael LEONARD	Heidelberg
14.	RIEMAN, John	Michael LIND	Lancaster
15.	REICHART, Adam	Caspar EGLE	do
16.	BECKER, Henry	Jacob LANDMESSER	Connestoga
17.	BLUM, George	Philip GLONINGER	Lebanon
18.	WERNEBURG, John	George SENEFF	Lancaster
19.	DEHN, Andreas	George STOVER	Cocalico
20.	HAWK, Paul	Timothy GREEN Esqr.	Hanover
21.	SIEBERT, George	Mark BIRD Esqr.	Reading
22.	SEITZ, Valentine		
23.	PETER, Jacob		
24.	MELCHIOR, Cilias	Richard LEMMON & Comp.	Baltimore
25.	HEROLD, Johannes		
26.	TRINNER, Conrad	Employed by Col. Curtiss GRUBB	[Cornwall]
27.	FISHER, John		
28.	FISHER, Conrad		
29.	KNOCHENHOUR, Herman		
30.	SUMMER, Conrad		
31.	GEBHART, George		
32.	ELIAS, Henry		
33.	FRICKER, Jacob		

GRENADIERS & YAGERS

#	Name		Place
1.	BINGAMAN, John	Christopher AMALONG	Lebanon
2.	RIEDE, John	Casper YOST	do
3.	HARTMAN, George	William BOWMAN Esqr.	Lancaster
4.	WERNER, Christoph		
5.	FOGEL, Philip	Anna FELTMAN	do
6.	MERGAL, Ludwig	Jas. MEASE Esqr.	do
7.	NIEMEYER, David	Jonas METZGER	do
8.	FLATBUSH, Frederick	Saml. WRIGHT	
9.	PAFF, Henry	Stephen HORNBERGAR	Hempfield
10.	MARDORFF, Anthony	Andreas KILLINGER	Hanover
11.	KOCH, John	Rudy STADLER	Earl T
12.	WHEELER, Augustus	Honbl. Wm. ATTLE Esqr.	
13.	STREITHOFF, Ludwig	Mark BIRD Esqr.	Reading
14.	RANSEL, Casimer of 28th Br. Regt.		
15.	WEYL, Henry	George ROSS Junr.	Lancaster
16.	DOHN, Charles	Richard LEMMON & Comp.	Baltimore

(1) "Farmed-out" prisoners taken at Trenton (Force Papers); there were 868 rank and file of the Rall brigade of Hessians taken at Trenton on December 26, 1776. [See THE BATTLE OF TRENTON by Samuel S. Smith 1965; p. 32] These men were marched to Pennsylvania; and after a short time in prison camps, 397 were "farmed-out" to work at various trades. This process took place between September 16 and November 20, 1777.

It is not known whether this list is of civilian or military origin. It is obvious that it was prepared by someone unfamiliar with the German language. For example, Heinrich Fahrenkamp is spelled Henry Farracamp, and Heinrich Wortmann is spelled Henry Wortman. Occasionally, a name appears twice. It is not known, for example, whether there were two men by the name of Henry Hattendorf or whether the same man was "farmed-out" once to Ludwick Uborn of Conestoga and once to Mr. James Ewing of York County.

An analysis was made of the von Lossberg regiment to determine the percentage of those soldiers "farmed-out" who chose to remain in America; and whether they were regulars or new recruits. Three returns of this regiment (for the years 1775, 1778, and 1783) were studied. These were published as a consolidated list in the doctoral dissertation of Robert Oakley Slagle at The American University in 1925, titled THE VON LOSSBERG REGIMENT.... Comparing Dr. Slagle's consolidated list with the von Lossberg "farmed-out" list it was found that only 20 of the 113 prisoners were on the consolidated list. It was concluded from this, that 93 of the 113 prisoners were new recruits who had been enlisted, and then captured between the date of the first return in 1775 and the second, in 1778. This bears out the Hessian High Command's contention that defections occurred mainly among the new recruits.

It was also noted that only six of those "farmed-out" prisoners were shown to have returned to their units by appearing on the 1783 portion of the Slagle consolidated list. This would indicate that only one in five of those who were "farmed-out" chose to return to their units.

(2) TOWNS AND/OR TOWNSHIPS MENTIONED IN PENNSYLVANIA WHERE HESSION SOLDIERS WERE "FARMED-OUT"

Bethel [township], Lebanon County
Cocalico [township], Lancaster County
Conestoga [township], Lancaster County (no longer extant)
Cornwall [township], Lebanon County
Donegal [township], Lancaster County
Earl [township], Lancaster County
Hanover [township], Dauphin County
Heidelberg [township], Lebanon County; also a Heidelberg, Township in Berks County.
Hellam [township], York County
Hempfield [township], Lancaster County
Lampeter [township], Lancaster County
Lancaster [town] Lancaster County
Lebanon [town or township], Lebanon County
Londonderry [township], Dauphin County
Manheim [town or township], Lancaster County
Manor [township], Lancaster County
Martic or Martick [township], Lancaster County
Mount Joy [township], Lancaster County
Paxton [township], Dauphin County
Rapho [township], Lancaster County
Reading [town], Berks County
Tulpenhocken [township], Berks County
Warwick [township], Lancaster County
Womelsdorf [town], Berks County
Wright's Ferry (now Columbia) [town], Lancaster County

These 18th century place names were identified by John R. Heisey, Director of Research, The Historical Society of York County, Pennsylvania.

PAPERS RELATING TO HESSIAN PRISONERS HELD IN DETENTION CAMPS IN PENNSYLVANIA

SHELBURNE PAPERS, vol. 69. p. 120-124.

The Address of Captain Bowen to the Brunswick and Hesse Hanau Prisoners of War — Reading July 30th 1782.

Whereas I am appointed to inlist such of you, as may wish to enter into the Service of America, and since I do not understand your Language and cannot converse with you, I have taken recourse to this method of informing you, of what I conceive to be the nature of your Situation.

The King of Great Britain has refused to support or exchange you, as prisoners of War, and the Congress of the United States of America, in Commiseration of the Sufferings occasioned by your long Confinement, has put it into your power to become free Citizens of this free and happy country, and for this Purpose have made you the following Propositions.

In the first place, Congress demands of you, the Sum of thirty Pounds, as a small consideration for your long support, or to find a person to pay that Sum for you.

The 2.d Consideration frees you from this Debt contracted for your Subsistence, by inlisting yourself into the American Service, and that in either case you do take the Oath of Allegiance to the United States. — If you should reply that you have already pledged your Allegiance to the King of Great Britain, I would have you consider that He has forfeited all pretentions to your Services, by refusing to acknowledge you to be prisoners of War, tho' taken in his Service, and by withdrawing or detaining your Subsistence Money, so indispensably necessary for your Support; and that under these Circumstances your Oaths are no longer binding on you or perhaps you may fear, should you become Subjects of these States or Soldiers in their Service, your Properties in Germany will be confiscated, to this I answer, we are not at War with your Princes, nor they with us, — they have sold your Services to the King of England for certain Sums of Money, and the fewer of you that return home during the War, the more Money must be paid by the Enemy into their Treasuries; for they have set a price on your heads, and cannot, under the present Circumstances, with the least shadow of Justice or any other pretences, forfeit your Estates.

FORM OF THE DISCHARGE

Know all Men by these Presents that   of   Regiment   a native of Germany and late a prisoner to the United States of America, has signified a Desire to become a free Citizen of the said States, I have therefore, by Virtue of the power in me vested, discharged him, and do by these Presents discharge the said   from being a Prisoner, but always on condition that he first takes the Oath of Allegiance hereunto subjoined.
        Given at Philadelphia, the   day of   1782.
        (signed)

COPY OF THE OATH

I the above named   do hereby   solemnly swear and declare, that I will bear faith and true Allegiance to the United States of America, and that I will demean myself as a good Subject of the same, So help me God.

SHELBURNE PAPERS, vol. 69. American Dispatches from Jan. 1783, no. 2. p. 117-119.

Extract of Instructions from the Honble the Minister of Finance of the United States of America, and the Honble the Secretary of the Board of War, dated at Philadelphia the 11th Day of July 1782.

The Minister of Finance and the Secretary of the Board of War, being duly authorized by the United States of America in Congress Assembled, have resolved that each and every of the German Prisoners of War, who will take the Oath of Allegiance to the said States, and pay unto me the Sum of Eighty Dollars, shall be discharged from confinement, be no longer considered as Prisoners of War, — and be intitled to the Rights and Priveleges of the free Citizens of the said States. "We do therefore fully authorize you to give a formal Discharge, a Copy of which is inclosed, unto each of the said Prisoners of War, who shall pay the sum of Eighty Dollars, and take the Oath of Allegiance annexed to his Discharge, before any Civil Magistrate commissioned to administer the same."

The underwritten is thus authorized to grant unto all such German Prisoners of War, encamped near Reading, who have complied with the said Instructions, such Discharges as are therein directed to be given.

He therefore gives notice to the prisoners of War aforesaid that he is to be found in the Town of Reading at the Inn of the Sign of General Washington, where he constantly attends to this Business.

He further informs all such prisoners of War, who may wish to enjoy the inestimable privilege of being free Citizens, and cannot pay the Sum of Eighty Dollars for their Discharge, that they are at liberty to enter into any Contract or Agreement which shall appear to be most advantageous for themselves with any Citizen of the State, who will advance that Sum of Money for any of them, provided the said Contract doth not exceed the Term of three years Servitude. — And in order that no Advantage be taken of the Prisoners Care will be had, that every Article of their Agreement, with the Person who shall advance the Money aforesaid, is specified and inserted in their Contracts or Indentures. And for their further Satisfaction and Instruction, a Copy of their Discharge and of the form of the Oath required of them is hereunto annexed.
Reading July 30th. 1782.   Signed, James Reed

CAPTAIN THOMAS BOWEN'S APPEAL TO PRISONERS

I wish you, Gentlemen, to consider the difference of the two Propositions, which will class you amongst the free people of America.

By the first you must pay money or become laborious Servants, and that to particular persons, who in all probability, when you are once bound, will shew you little Humanity, as is already the case.

By the second, you are to continue in that Honorable Profession of a Soldier, under the banners of that magnanimous Commander General Washington, defending the Cause of liberty and the Rights of Humanity. — Shall Veteran Soldiers then, trained in the Art of War; prefer a mean Servitude without pay and for no less a term than three years, to the glorious Profession of Arms? — No, — Gentlemen, come to me, and such of you as will enter into the Service shall, instead of paying money, receive Eight Dollars to drink a Health to Congress; and instead of serving a farmer three years for nothing, be taken into immediate Pay, have good Quarters, and every thing else necessary to equip a Gentleman Soldier, and if you will enrol yourselves to serve during the War, which to all appearances will not continue three years longer, you shall be intitled to one Hundred acres of good Land in America, when you may enjoy yourselves with your Offspring under your own Vine and Fig Tree, saying, I have deserted the Services of a tyrannick King for those of a free and rising State — my recompense is Liberty and the Necessaries of Life, both which Blessings, I can now bequeath to my Posterity.

I do not insinuate that you are compelled to accept one or other Propositions already mentioned, nor is it known what the Consequences of an obstinate refusal of either may be, yet notwithstanding I am free in giving you my opinions, that if you refuse to accept of these Propositions, widently [sic] calculated to promote your Welfare; you will have enjoyed the best part of your liberty; a liberty not known to other Prisoners of War, and which I have been at great pains in procuring for you, as you were left under my care and protection.

Gentlemen, I believe you are very sensible that I have at all times had great pleasure in doing every thing in my power to make your Confinement as easy as the nature of the Case would admit, — I shall continue to treat you as formally, and those amongst you who may accept the offers made by Congress, which I am authorized to lay before you, shall find in me a friend and Protector.
(Signed) Thomas Bartholomeus Bowen,
5th Pennsylvania Regiment, recruiting
officer of the German Prisoners of War.
To the German Prisoners of War, encamped near Reading.
NB. Such non Commissioned Officers as shall first enter, will retain their Rank in the proportion of four Serjeants to every hundred Men.

INDEX

Appendix material is not indexed. The words America or Americans, Germany or Germans, Hessians, Great Britain or British may be found on almost every page, and are not indexed. In the text, German names are printed as they were found in the original manuscript. For example: Ditfurth, Dittfurth or Dittfourth are variations. In indexing, we have chosen the most common spelling or the one appearing first.

A

Altonaer-Zeitung 8
Amboy, N.J. 17
Anhalt-Zerbst 5
Annapolis, Md. 17
Anspach-Bayreuth 5, 7, 12, 20
Archer's Hope Plantation 18
Ashley River 18
Atlantic Neptune 15, 17
Augsburgische-Postzeitung 11, 13

B

Baltimore, Md. 17
Bar, Confederacy of 7
Bardeleben, Lt. von Heinrich 13, 20, 22
Barren Island 15
Bauer, Q.M. Carl 14, 16, 18, 22, 26, 29, 33
Baur, Franz August 35
Baurmeister, Maj. Carl Leopold 8-11, 15, 17, 23, 29, 31, 33-36
Bavia Gate 32
Bedlow's Island 15
Benning, Von (regt.) 31
Bennington, Vt. 26
Bordentown, N.J. 30
Bose, Von (regt.) 11, 35
Boston, Mass. 34
Boudinot, Elias 11
Bourgoyne, Gen. John 26
Broadway 15
Bremerlche, Ger. 6
Bristol Ferry 32
Bristol, R.I. 33
Brooklyn, N.Y. 10
Brunswick 5, 11, 12
Bunkershill, Fort (N.Y.) 16

C

Cadiz 13
Calhoun Street 18
Canada 23
Carl II, Duke 12
Carl Wilhelm Ferdinand, Prince 12
Carleton, Lt. Gen. Guy 9
Carpenters Hall 16
Cassel, Ger. 6, 8, 9, 10, 15, 16, 25, 29, 34
Charleston, S.C. 10, 18, 19, 23, 26
Charming Nancy (ship) 7
Cherokee Indians 27
Chesapeake Bay 18
Chickasaw Indians 27
Clarke, Brig. Gen. Alured 10, 11
Clinton, Lt. Gen. Henry 9, 23, 25, 30, 32
Cochenhausen, Lt. Col. Johann Friedrich von 8, 35
College Creek 18
Columbia Magazine 16
Combined Battalion 23
Connecticut 35
Connecticut Farms, N.J. 31
Cooper River 18
Cornwall Iron Works 24
Cornwallis, Gen. Charles 11, 23, 25, 35

D

De Corps, (regt.) 6, 8, 9, 14, 16
Delaware River 16, 21
Dettingen, Ger. 12
Diemar, Von (regt.) 6
Dincklage, Lt. Col. August von 14-18, 21, 26, 28, 29, 30, 34
Dittfurth, von (regt.) 9, 15, 31
Dittfurth, Lt. Gen. von 29
Donop, Col. Carl Emil Ulrich von 9, 17, 25, 30
Dordrecht, Neth. 8
Dumphries, Va. 17

E

Eagle (ship) 4
East River 15
Egg Harbor, N.J. 23
Elizabethtown, N.J. 31, 32

Elk Ferry, Md. 9, 21
English Channel 6, 7
Erb Prinz (regt.) 11, 35
Eschwege, Capt. Friedrich von 25
Ewald, Capt. Johann (von) 7, 14, 19, 20, 22, 23-26, 28, 29, 31, 32

F

Fenner, Capt. H.C. 7
Fischer, Capt. Johann Jacob 25
Flushing, L.I. 34
Ford, Col. Jacob 18
Ford, Timothy 18
France 34, 35
Franklin, Dr. Benjamin 35
Freehold, N.J. 19
Friedrich II, Landgrave 5-8, 12, 20, 26
Friedrich-August, Prince 5
Friedrich, Prince 5

G

Galloway, Joseph 23
George, Fort 16
George II, King 12, 20
George III, King 5, 12, 21
Georgia 14
Gerber, Capt. Claudius 31
German, Chronicle 21
Germanic Review 7
Gloucester, Va. 23
Gneisenau, Cadet Neidhardt von 15
Goettingen, Ger. 14, 17, 20
Gohr, Lt. Gen. von 7
Gosen, Maj. Gen. David Uphriam von 11
Gotha, Ger. 7
Governor's Island 15
Grubb, Col. Curtiss 24
Guard (Regt.) 6, 25

H

Hackensack, N.J. 23
Halifax, N.S. 4, 7, 8
Hampton Roads 9
Hannover, Duke of 7
Hanover, Ger. 16
Hatzfeld, Col. von 7
Heister, Lt. Gen. Leopold von 15, 21, 25
Henkelmann, Lt. Johannes Heinrich 28, 29, 31
Hesse, Ger. 6, 7, 25, 36
Hesse-Cassel 5, 6, 7, 12, 20
Hesse-Hanau 5, 7, 11, 20
Hesse-Hanau Free-Corps 31
Heusser, Q.M. Georg Ludwig Christian 13, 21, 29
Hinrichs, Capt. Johann 13, 14, 17, 20, 21, 24, 27, 30, 31, 33, 34
Holland 10
Howe, Admiral Richard 4
Howe, Lt. Gen. William 9, 23, 30
Hudson River 15
Huyne, von (regt.) 15, 28
Huyne, Maj. Gen. Johann Christoph von 32

I

Independence Hall 16, 17

J

Jackson, Maj. William 11
Jaeger (Corps.) 6, 7, 9, 10, 13, 20, 22
James River 18
Jena, Ger. 7
Jungkenn, Baron von 7, 14, 15, 21, 25, 28, 34

K

Kabale und Liebe 12
Kalm, Peter 20
Karl Alexander, Markgrave 5
Karlshafen 8
Kean, Mrs. John 32
Kings Bridge 20
Kings College 15
King Street 18
Kleinschmidt, Ens. 10
Kleinschmidt, Q.M. Friedrich Jacob 18, 27, 28, 30, 31, 34
Knoblauch, von (regt.) 10
Knoblauch, Maj. Gen. Hans 7
Knyphausen, von (regt.) 10, 11, 22, 23
Knyphausen, Lt. Gen. Wilhelm 9, 17, 31, 32, 34
Koehler, (batt.) 13, 14
Koester, Field-Chaplain 25
Krug, Capt. Georg 25
Kuemmel, Field-Chaplain Heinrich 15

L

Lafayette, Marquis de 18
Lancaster, Pa. 10, 24
Landgraf (or Landgrave Regt.) 9, 10, 31
Lebanon, Pa. 10
Lee, Fort 14
Leib (regt.) 31
Leslie, Maj. Gen. Alexander 9, 10
Liberty Hall 32
Library Company 16
Lincoln, Gen. Benjamin 23
Lith, Baron Von der 20
Livingston, Peter Van Brugh 32
Livingston, Susan 31, 32
Livingston, William 31, 32
London 8, 34
Long Island 14, 15, 21, 22, 30
Loos, Col. Johann August von 8, 22
Lossberg (Alt-Regt.) 8, 13, 17
Lossberg, Lt. Gen. Friedrich Wilhelm von 8, 9, 10, 11, 33
Lotheisen, Q.M. 16, 20
Lower-Creek Indians 26, 27

M

Malsburg, Capt. Friedrich von der 15, 19, 21, 22, 24, 27, 28, 30, 31, 34
Manhattan Island 14, 15
Marburg, Ger. 29
Martin, Capt. Reinhard Jacob 22
Martini, Capt. Melchior 15
Maryland 23, 24
Meeting Street 18
Meiningen, Ger. 7
Minnigerode, von (regt.) 19
Mirbach, von (regt.) 9, 21
Monmouth, Battle of 20
Morristown, N.J. 18
Morristown Natl. Hist. Park 18
Muenchhausen, Capt. Baron Friedrich Ernst von 15, 30
Munchner-Zeitung 13
Munich, Ger. 13

N

New Brunswick, N.J. 22
New England 34, 36
New Jersey 10, 11, 13, 14, 21, 23, 24, 27, 30, 31, 32
New Jersey Highlands 13
Newport, R.I. 19, 27
New York 5, 8, 10, 15, 16, 17, 19, 21-24, 31-34, 36
New York Bay 4, 13
North Carolina 25
Nova Scotia 23
Nurenberg, Ger. 24
Nutten Island 15

O

Oldenburg (regt.) 14
Oreilly, Capt. Maximilian Wilhelm 30, 31

P

Paris 10
Payne, David M. 32
Penn, Count 21
Pennsylvania 10, 11, 21, 23, 24, 28, 36
Philadelphia 10, 11, 16, 17, 19, 21-24, 29, 31, 33-36
Phillips, Gen. William 25
Philosophical Society 16
Piel, Lt. Jacob 17
Point Bridge 19
Porbeck, von (regt.) 9, 31
Portsmouth, Va. 23
Potomac River 17
Prescott, Gen. Richard 32, 34
Prevost, Gen. Augustine 23
Prince Carl (regt.) 25
Prince Hereditary (regt.) 13
Princeton, N.J. 36
Providence, R.I. 28
Puy, Lt. Col. du 11, 29

Q

Quantico River 17
Queen's River 18

R

Rall, Col. Johann Gottlieb 22
Reading, Pa. 10, 23
Regensburg, Ger. 15
Reuting, Capt. Henrich Wilhelm 31

Rheinfels, Ger. 8
Rhode Island 15, 32, 33, 35
Ritter, Lt. 17
Robertson, Capt. Lt. Archibald 4
Rochambeau, Gen. Donatien Vimeur 35
Rockingham 36
Rocky Hill, N.J. 36
Roll, Capt. Herman Christian 35
Romulus (ship) 9
Rueffer, Lt. 21

S

St. Espirit Church 17
St. George's Chapel 16
St. Paul's Church 15, 16
Sandy Hook 4, 5
Sandy Hook Bay 4, 13
Sandy Hook Light House 15
Sartorius, Q.M. 13
Savannah, Ga. 10, 19, 22, 33
Schallern, Col. Ludwig von 7
Scheer, Maj. 11
Schiller, Friedrich 12
Schloezer, August Ludwig 14, 17, 20, 34
Schlotheim, von (regt.) 6
Schotten, Lt. Friedrich Andreas 21
Schubarth, Christian Daniel 21
Schuylkill River 16, 21
Seimsen 25
Seitz, von (Regt.) 7, 31
Seume, Johann Gottfried 7
South Carolina 14, 23, 33, 34

Spangenberg, Ens. 35
Spotswood, N.J. 14
Stanwix, Fort 26
Staten Island 4, 5, 11, 13, 14, 15, 31, 32
Stein, Dr. 8
Stillwater, N.Y. 26
Stirling, Brig. Gen. Thomas 31
Strasser, Ens. 9
Sullivan, Brig. Gen. John 21
Susquehannah River 29

T

Tarrytown, N.Y. 22
Taylor, M. 32
Tea Water Fountain 16
Thames Street 19
Thirty-Eighth British (regt.) 31
Thirty-Seventh British (regt.) 31
Thurston, Rev. Charles M. 17
Tischbein, Jr. 30
Tischbein, Johann Heinrich (Sr.) 12
Trenton, N.J. 10, 14, 17, 19, 22, 23, 24, 29, 30, 31
Trinity Church (N.Y.) 17
Trinity Church (Newport, R.I.) 19

U

Uhlendorf, Bernhard A. 7

V

Valley Forge 29, 34
Vienna, Aus. 7

Virginia 20, 22, 24, 25, 29
Vockroth, Ens. 9

W

Waldeck 5, 7
Wall Street Presbyterian 17
Washington, Fort 22
Washington, Gen. George 23, 29, 34, 36
Washington, Mrs. Martha 32
Wernicke, Lt. 31
Weser River 8
West Indies 23
Westphalia 14
West Point 36
Wiederholt, Lt. Andreas 19, 24, 26, 28, 29
Wilhelm, Duke 5
Wilhelmshoehe Castle 8
Williamsburg, Va. 18, 20
Winchester, Va. 17
Wissenbach, von (regt.) 9
Woellwarth, von (regt.) 10
Wuerzburg 7
Wurmb, Lt. Col. Friedrich Wilhelm von 8, 31, 32
Wurmb, Col. Ludwig Johann Adolph 7, 10, 20, 33, 34, 36

Y

York, Pa. 10
Yorktown, Va. 20, 23, 25, 35, 36

Z

Ziegenhain, Fort 7, 8

7.95